D1191548

JULIAN THE APOSTATE

JULIAN
THE APOSTATE

G. W. Bowersock

Harvard University Press
Cambridge, Massachusetts
1978

Library of Congress Cataloging in Publication Data

Bowersock, Glen Warren.
    Julian the Apostate.

    Bibliography: p.
    Includes index.
    1. Julianus, Apostata, Emperor of Rome, 331–363.
2. Roman emperors – Biography.   I.   Title.
DG317.B68   937'.08'0924 [B]   77–22769
ISBN 0–674–48881–4

1–10–79

Printed in Great Britain

Contents

List of Illustrations

Acknowledgments

I T is a pleasure to express my indebtedness to the members of the Julian seminar which I conducted at Harvard in the spring of 1976. No scholar could have wished for more alert and competent critics. I have profited especially from Donald McCabe's views of Julian's policy toward the Christians.

To Professor Hugh Lloyd-Jones I am deeply grateful for encouraging me to write this volume. It is a particular pleasure to be able to present my interpretation of Julian with so congenial a publisher, and I have endeavoured to provide sufficient documentation to make it possible for readers to investigate the basic sources and the principal matters of scholarly controversy. For discussion and criticism I have also to express my thanks to Professors T. D. Barnes, C. P. Jones, and Irfan Shahîd. I owe a special debt to Professor François Paschoud for generously making available to me the typescript of his forthcoming annotations on the third book of Zosimus in the Collection Budé. For the valuable opportunity to communicate my views on Edward Gibbon's important treatment of Julian in the *Decline and Fall* I am grateful to Professor Pierre Ducrey, who kindly invited me to participate in the Colloque Gibbon at Lausanne in June of 1976. Finally, I wish to thank Dr Cornelius Vermeule and Dr William Metcalf for their prompt courtesy in making available for publication photographs of coins in the collections of the Museum of Fine Arts, Boston, and the American Numismatic Society respectively.

My reading of Gibbon and of Cavafy's seven matchless poems on Julian has substantially influenced my understanding of the ancient sources, which both men knew better than most. It is for this reason that I have prefaced the present study with excerpts from those two great writers. My deepest debt is to them.

G.W.B.

In the caverns of Ephesus and Eleusis the mind of Julian was penetrated with sincere, deep, and unalterable enthusiasm; though he might sometimes exhibit the vicissitudes of pious fraud and hypocrisy which may be observed, or at least suspected, in the characters of the most conscientious fanatics.

He affected to pity the unhappy Christians, who were mistaken in the most important object of their lives; but his pity was degraded by contempt, his contempt was embittered by hatred; and the sentiments of Julian were expressed in a style of sarcastic wit, which inflicts a deep and deadly wound whenever it issues from the mouth of a sovereign.

I have endeavoured faithfully to represent the artful system by which Julian proposed to obtain the effects, without incurring the guilt or reproach, of persecution. But if the deadly spirit of fanaticism perverted the heart and understanding of a virtuous prince, it must, at the same time, be confessed, that the real sufferings of the Christians were inflamed and magnified by human passions and religious enthusiasm.

Edward Gibbon, *Decline and Fall,* ch. 23

JULIAN AND THE ANTIOCHENES

*Neither the letter C, they say, nor the letter K had ever
harmed the city . . . We, finding interpreters . . . learned
that these are the initial letters of names, the first of
Christ and the second of Konstantios.*

Julian, *Misopogon*

How could they ever give up
their beautiful way of life, the range
of their daily pleasures, their brilliant theatre
which consummated a union between Art
and the erotic proclivities of the flesh?

Immoral to a degree—and probably more than a degree—
they certainly were. But they had the satisfaction that their life
was the notorious life of Antioch,
delectable, in absolute good taste.

To give up all this, indeed, for what?

His hot air about the false gods,
his boring self-advertisement,
his childish fear of the theatre,
his graceless prudery, his ridiculous beard.

O certainly they preferred C,
certainly they preferred K—a hundred times over.

C. P. Cavafy (translated by E. Keeley and P. Sherrard)

Prologue

THE life and reign of the emperor Julian were both short. He died in his early thirties and reigned alone for just over a year and a half. The outline of his public career is simple: about five and a half years as commander in Gaul where he was finally proclaimed emperor by his troops, a dramatic march to the east to confront his rival Constantius (who died opportunely), six months in Constantinople, nine turbulent months in Antioch, an unsuccessful campaign against the Persians. Yet Julian is without question one of antiquity's most enigmatic and compelling figures. He attempted the impossible by restoring for a moment the pagan gods to their former primacy, a feat which horrified the Christians and probably perplexed rather than inspired the majority of surviving pagans.

Julian was a man of action and at the same time a man whose spiritual life brought him close to several of the most extreme wonder-workers of his age. He was imbued with the mysteries of Neo-Platonism and yet, as a recent study has taught us,[1] had little of importance to contribute to serious philosophy. The Neo-Platonic background is important for Julian only in the study of his emotional life and of those self-revelations which he not very artfully concealed in his reflective treatises.

The pages which follow constitute an exploration of the available evidence in search of the real, the historical Julian. While most of the book follows a roughly chronological order, a strictly biographical form from birth to death has not been imposed because it is quite unmanageable. The interpretation of events in one part of Julian's life cannot be made without reference to what we know of other parts. This is especially true for the years of his youth, which even in the contemporary sources are viewed from the perspective of what happened to him later. Therefore, allusions to later events are freely included in the dis-

---

[1] R. T. Wallis, *Neoplatonism* (1972), p. 96.

cussion of earlier ones. And a comprehensive essay on Julian's personality is presented before the detailed narrative in the hope of giving it more substance and credibility.

Anyone who believes that he can write an authoritative biography of Julian, with everything tidily in place from beginning to end, is deluding himself. The historian can only grope toward the facts about the man and his reign, but the groping is its own reward.

CHAPTER ONE

Approaching the Reign

OF the great figures of antiquity few are so abundantly documented and few so legendary as the emperor Julian. Perhaps only
Alexander the Great, whom Julian admired, exerts a comparable
fascination; but Alexander's career can more readily encourage
flights of fantasy because the documentation is less good. With
Julian the material is so abundant that novelists and dramatists,
not to mention historians, have to choose from a wide variety of
important witnesses who represent a spectrum of prejudices and
preconceptions about the emperor. In the twentieth century it is
by no means easy to surmount all the panegyric and obloquy
which has for so long been lavished upon Julian and to draw from
the evidence of antiquity its hidden truth. One must clear out the
impressions that linger from reading fictional masterworks like
those of Gore Vidal or Ibsen or Merezhkovsky or Rhangavis.[1]
One must alike reject, firmly and dispassionately, the lonely hero
struggling against the onslaught of corrupt Christianity, the

[1] For a good survey of the influence of Julian upon writers of imaginative
literature, see R. Browning, *The Emperor Julian* (1975), chapter 11, from which,
however, the Julian poems of Cavafy are regrettably absent. It should perhaps be
said here that the present interpretation of Julian and his career differs from
Browning's in attending explicitly to the ancient testimony and in sketching a
portrait quite unlike his. I am in full agreement with Browning's general view of
late antique history as outlined in his first chapter, but of Julian he says, 'He was a
tragic figure, a man of infinite promise, cut off before his prime. An American
student once compared him with President John F. Kennedy. The comparison
will not bear close analysis. But the feeling behind it suggests why Julian became
the subject of legend within a few years of his death.' (p. xii, cf. p. 235). When
Julian died, all Christians and many pagans received the news with relief. The
comparison with Kennedy seems to me totally unilluminating. The reader will
judge.

apostate manipulated by the forces of evil, and the courageous friend of the Jews. Julian was none of these.

In less than a century after he died the legends which had gathered around this emperor's short reign of nineteen months had already eclipsed the authentic memorials which survived from his own day. A clutch of church historians, orthodox and unorthodox, compounded into narrative form the rumours, gossip, and invective of half a century or more. It was not that these writers—Philostorgius, Rufinus, Socrates, Theodoret, and Sozomen—did not have access to reliable reports conserved in histories now lost to us, as well as to the speeches and letters we still read. It was rather the indiscriminate blending of fact with fiction which produced the unhistorical amalgam we see in the mediaeval and modern Julian. An early and absorbing example of this creation can be observed in the long romance of Julian that survives in Syriac from the Christian literature of the Near East. No one will mistake fiction for fact in that narrative: the voice from heaven, for instance, which precedes the appearance of the fatal lance on the battlefield where Julian died belongs manifestly to the realm of legend. But in earlier, less advanced traditions about Julian the reliability of what is told is not always so obvious.

The historian must cut his way back through the luxuriant growth of later ages to the testimony and traditions of Julian's own time, the fourth century A.D. The effort is not without its own intrinsic interest, since the later accretions can sometimes be significant indications of what was there before. And, of course, once the goal is reached, once the contemporary witnesses are uncovered and on show, the judicious critic must then decide what they are worth. It is no simple matter to get at the reign of Julian. The emperor and his work have to be approached circumspectly.

The extant ecclesiastical historians of the fifth century A.D. were heirs to the invective of two eloquent fathers of the Church, Gregory of Nazianzus (a contemporary of Julian) and John Chrysostom (of the following generation.) What they recorded or surmised was normally reproduced by the historians of the next century, and what they omitted was likely to be omitted. Yet the historian Socrates took the trouble to consult and to cite a pagan writer like Libanius of Antioch; and Philostorgius, not so ready, because of his unorthodox Eunomian persuasion, to perpetuate orthodox views, looked elsewhere for sources such as the history, now lost, by Eunapius of Sardis.[2] As for Rufinus, he appears to have availed himself of a continuation of Eusebius' Ecclesiastical History by a certain Gelasius of Palestinian Caesarea.[3] Sozomen wrote later with Socrates' work before him, but he did not hesitate to supplement it when he could. Ironically after the whole parade of Christian historians there came in the early sixth century the pagan Zosimus, whose history included nearly an entire book devoted to Julian. That book, according to the Byzantine patriarch Photius,[4] was no more than an epitome of the history by Eunapius of Sardis. Therefore, from the sixth century we acquire a control on earlier writers who used Eunapius—like the Eunomian Philostorgius.

In this way the various accounts can be seen to turn back on themselves, to have interrelationships and distinctive differences at the same time. No one account can be entirely rejected or entirely trusted. At each point it is worth no more and no less than the accounts from which it is drawn. Accordingly it is necessary to review and to assess the original materials, both surviving and lost. To these materials the modern historian, unlike the ancient, will add the precious evidence of coins, inscriptions, and edicts. Only by a careful process of screening and review can one ultimately discern the emperor as he was.

If we consider the contemporary literary evidence for Julian, three major sources are immediately apparent. These are the writings of the emperor himself, certain speeches of the sophist

---

[2] Cf. Philostorgius, *Kirchengeschichte*, ed. J. Bidez, 2nd ed. by F. Winkelmann (1972), pp. cxxxviii–cxxxix.

[3] On Gelasius of Caesarea, known through the writings of Gelasius of Cyzicus, see F. Winkelmann, *Untersuchungen zur Kirchengeschichte des Gelasios von Kaisareia* (1965); and *Byzantinoslavica* 27 (1966), 104 ff.

[4] Photius, *Biblioth*. cod. 98, p. 84 Bk.

Libanius, and the invective of the Cappadocian father, Gregory of Nazianzus.

The voluminous works of Julian—speeches, satires and letters —mirror the man in his political, religious, and military activities. Some of the pieces were designed for public consumption, like the Panegyrics to Constantius and Eusebia or the notorious apology to the Athenians in which Julian attempted to justify his revolt. Others, while aimed at the public, expose the passions of the author. Such is the *Misopogon* addressed to the people of Antioch. Some writings, especially the letters and the religious essays, offer a remarkable view of the inner life and deeply rooted convictions of Julian.

All his writings, taken together, provide an insight into character and disposition such as can be had for no other classical figure apart from Cicero. Yet such was the tradition of historiography in antiquity that this fundamental evidence for Julian was largely ignored in subsequent accounts of his reign. No enemy of the emperor and no friend, however voluble, undertook to use his many writings, except for the letter to the Athenians and the *Misopogon*, to present a more convincing portrait. His works did not infect the tradition which grew up around him, and often therefore they can serve to control the tradition itself.

The sophist of Syrian Antioch, Libanius, was never short of words. His vast production brilliantly illumines the Near Eastern society of his age, and the friendship he formed with Julian underlies a series of important discourses which touch upon the life and aims of that emperor.[5] Libanius saluted his monarch in studied addresses on the occasion of Julian's arrival in Antioch as well as later at the inception of the next consular year. He petitioned Julian, he advised the citizens to have regard for the emperor's anger, and he mourned his death. Libanius' funeral speech for Julian is nothing less than a full, if highly partisan, biography of his friend. This work and a subsequent one on

[5] A. F. Norman has recently published an invaluable edition of these discourses in the first volume of Libanius to appear in the Loeb Classical Library (1969). Norman's translation, introduction, and notes have now made Julian's reign far more accessible to modern readers.

divine vengeance for Julian's death are invaluable sources for the facts and traditions that circulated soon after the brief reign. Libanius undoubtedly knew things he chose to omit, but nowhere can he be convicted of outright falsification of items he chose to include. He was a pagan and a panegyrist, capable of putting untenable constructions upon the truth; but he was not a liar. His testimony takes second place only to that of Julian himself.

Gregory, the Arian bishop from Cappadocian Nazianzus, was as deeply prejudiced as Libanius, but on the other side. He was Julian's schoolmate at Athens, and he watched that scholarly scion of the house of Constantine with great care. His later claims to have foreseen the menace which would threaten the Christian establishment may be dismissed as wishful thinking in retrospect, but there is nothing to discredit the details of which he was an eyewitness. Naturally as emperor Julian kept himself far from Gregory. Yet Gregory was an intelligent recipient of facts and gossip that were current, so that the denunciations he wrote shortly after Julian's death constitute a valuable repository of early Christian traditions. As a witness Gregory is perceptive as well as passionately hostile, for he shared the Hellenic heritage which Julian promoted. Gregory refused to accept the transmutation of the cultural Hellenism he cherished into a religion he could not tolerate.[6]

With Julian himself, Libanius, and Gregory we have three substantial, contemporary sources for the reign. A panegyric, delivered by the consul Claudius Mamertinus on the first day of January 362, may be added to the contemporary dossier. This work demonstrates by its affirmations of the opposite what criticisms were being levelled at Julian at that moment. It well illustrates the direction of imperial propaganda at the outset of his reign as sole emperor. The literary texts of his own time, together with the imperial edicts which survive in the Theodosian Code, form a secure basis for the study of Julian. Only the

---

[6] Cf. Greg. Naz., *orat.* 4.5 (Migne, *PG* 35.536A–B) and 4.103 (Migne, *PG* 637B–640A). Also Rosemary Radford Ruether, *Gregory of Nazianzus: Rhetor and Philosopher* (1969), pp. 163–4.

contemporary coins and inscriptions have comparable authority. It will be observed that none of this material provides a narrative account of the emperor and his reign, and it is perhaps for this reason that many historians, in the struggle to clear out the tangle of sources from various periods, have turned with relief to the year-by-year story told in Latin by Ammianus Marcellinus.[7]

In attempts to get at Julian's reign, the history of Ammianus seemed a godsend. This writer had, after all, served under Julian in Gaul when the future emperor was still Caesar, and it was evident that Ammianus had also been present on the catastrophic Persian expedition at the end of Julian's career. Moreover, Ammianus was a native of Syrian Antioch and could readily grasp the problems which confronted Julian there. He wrote as a sober and discerning historian who explicitly repudiated trivia in favour of what he considered history's high places (*celsitudines*).[8] Here was an eye-witness who provided a narrative account, studded (in the fashion of ancient historiography) with speeches and letters in direct quotation. Ammianus appeared to be both authoritative and convenient. Hence from the days of the Abbé de la Bléterie down to the present the history of Ammianus has provided the foundation, and sometimes the whole edifice, for historians of the emperor Julian.[9] Ammianus' impartiality and integrity seemed guaranteed by the adverse judgments which he occasionally passed on a man whom in general he considered a model of the human virtues.

It was not surprising that those who tried to exploit the writings of Julian, Libanius, and Gregory within a framework fixed by Ammianus produced a discordant and unintegrated version of Julian's reign. This was the problem of Gibbon's memorable chapters, which even reproduce the speeches in Ammianus as authentic utterances of the emperor. Yet these were certainly the

[7] For Ammianus, see E. A. Thompson, *The Historical Work of Ammianus Marcellinus* (1947).

[8] Amm. Marc. 26.1.1.

[9] The *Vie de Julien* of the Abbé de la Bléterie is still worth reading. It was first published anonymously at Amsterdam in 1735 and then reprinted at Paris, with his name, in 1746. Gibbon knew this biography intimately.

work of the historian, like the speeches that regularly appeared in ancient historiography from Herodotus onward. The Belgian scholar Joseph Bidez, who did so much admirable work on Julian in the twentieth century, was still not free of Ammianus. He included in his publication of Julian's letters a text given by Ammianus as an adornment to his narrative. The existence of a running account of Julian and his reign by an eastern officer who had served under him has been too seductive. Ammianus did not write in the years immediately after the reign but some three decades later. And he was an ambitious historian, not merely putting down his personal recollections for the benefit of later historians but creating a work of art.

It has long been noticed that Ammianus' text shows striking parallels for the reign of Julian with the history of Zosimus, who wrote over a century later. The notion of a Latin source for the Greek historian has never been seriously countenanced for good reason, and in the last century several hypotheses have been advanced to explain the relation between the two historians. The crucial fact—and it cannot be avoided—is the dependence of Zosimus upon the history, now lost, by Eunapius of Sardis. This fact is given unambiguously, as we have already noted, by the patriarch Photius, who was able to compare both an early and a later edition of Eunapius' work with two editions of Zosimus' history. Photius makes it plain that Zosimus is little more than an epitomator of Eunapius. That being so, Eunapius must be the basis of the parallels between Zosimus and Ammianus. Since chronology precludes Eunapius' use of Ammianus, it is immediately apparent that Ammianus must have used Eunapius;[10] nor is

---

[10] Ammianus' use of Eunapius is crucial. Cf. W. R. Chalmers, *Classical Quarterly* n.s. 10 (1960), 152 ff.; T. D. Barnes, *Classical Philology* 71 (1976), 266–267; G. W. Bowersock, *Gibbon et Rome* (1977), pp. 207–8. See also *Oxford Classical Dictionary*, 2nd edition (1970), s.v. Ammianus. In his *Cinq études sur Zosime* (1976), pp. 177–9, François Paschoud considers that Ammianus may have had direct access to Oribasius' memoir. Elaborating on his article in *Classical Philology*, T. D. Barnes argues persuasively in his forthcoming book, *The Sources of the Historia Augusta*, chapter 9, that the first edition of Eunapius' *History* ended with the Battle of Adrianople in 378, rather than 395 (as previously assumed). This is an improvement on Chalmers' suggestions, which presupposed a date of 395 (after Ammianus had written his work). Chalmers had therefore to

this at all remarkable since Ammianus, as a native of Antioch, knew Greek from childhood, and the work of Eunapius has particular claim to a historian's attention.

Eunapius wrote his history with the aid of a memoir written especially for him by Julian's personal physician and friend, Oribasius. It is clear from Eunapius' remarks that Oribasius wrote his memoir precisely to elicit the history, and it is now equally clear that Eunapius had completed the first edition of his work not—as once thought—just after 395, too late for Ammianus, but by about 380, in plenty of time for the historian of Antioch to digest and paraphrase what he found there. There is no indication anywhere that Oribasius ever intended his notes for anyone other than Eunapius. There is no evidence that they survived or circulated, and with Eunapius' work available to Ammianus there is no need to postulate that they did.

The history of Eunapius was no less seductive to historians like Ammianus or Zosimus than Ammianus' own history has been to modern historians. It provided a running narrative. Manifestly dependent upon the reports of one of Julian's few intimate and constant companions up to the night of his death, Eunapius' history can legitimately claim an importance and authority not unlike that of Libanius or Gregory. Its loss is a major gap in the Julianic tradition, although several remarks in Eunapius' surviving *Lives of the Sophists* have long given glimpses of the privileged information to which he had access. Neither Oribasius nor Eunapius were impartial, any more than Libanius or Gregory—or Julian himself, for that matter. But they take us directly back to the reign in a way that Ammianus does not. Eyewitness and participant, Ammianus nevertheless wrote largely at second-hand, preferring as a self-conscious artistic historian to make his mosaic from a variety of sources, used even where he had personal knowledge. This was nothing new in Roman letters: Sallust had done the same when he wrote about North Africa in his monograph on the war with Jugurtha.

---

assume, unreasonably (as Paschoud points out), prior publication of parts of the *History* of Eunapius.

The evidence of Eunapius is therefore significant. Wh[
can be disengaged from texts that survive, it deserves a p[...
comparable to that accorded Libanius and Gregory. Apart from
Ammianus, Zosimus, and Eunapius' own *Lives of the Sophists,*
traces of the History have also been detected in Philostorgius'
Ecclesiastical History and in the Byzantine narrative of Zonaras.
Other church historians appear as innocent of the work of the
pagan Eunapius as they are of the works of Julian.

The quest for the historical Julian leads also to some Latin
epitomators who wrote soon after the emperor's death and had
access to contemporary information. Of these the concise universal historian, Eutropius, takes pride of place since he wrote
only six years after the fateful Persian campaign and by his own
clear statement served on it.[11] More difficult to assess is the notice
assigned to Julian by Festus in his *Breviarium,* written just a few
years after Eutropius' book. Although close in time to Julian's
reign, Festus reports a tradition which is demonstrably untrue
and must derive from the channels of rumour that were so quickly
clogged when Julian died. Something similar seems to be the
case for the notice in Jerome's ecclesiastical chronicle, which has a
striking affinity to Festus' *Breviarium* in the account of Julian.
The anonymous author of the epitome on the Caesars, writing
in the late fourth century, belongs equally in the untrustworthy
line of Festus and Jerome. There is little to justify the conclusion
that either of the two Latin writers after Festus made any use of
the Greek history of Eunapius, even though his work might by
then have been available to them.

One Christian contemporary of Julian, totally neglected by
the ancient purveyors of history and legend, must not be neglected
here. Like Gregory he exulted in the apostate's death and gave
utterance to his jubilation. He is Ephraem of Nisibis in Mesopotamia, who was expelled from his city along with his compatriots under the terms of Jovian's peace treaty with the Persians
after the failure of Julian's campaign. Ephraem settled in Edessa,
where he continued to pour out Syriac verse of a quality

[11] Eutropius 10.16: . . . *cui expeditioni ego quoque interfui.*

unmatched before or since. Among his compositions are four astonishingly vivid and intense invectives against Julian.[12] Ephraem saw the emperor's corpse as it lay outside the walls of Nisibis during Jovian's retreat. He saw the Persian standard hoisted over his city. In his verses he tells all this along with the stories he had heard about Julian's policies and the details of his death. Ephraem is a valuable witness. He is, for example, the only ancient writer to make references to the still unexplained coinage which Julian issued with the representation of a bull and two stars.[13] Published for the first time in the nineteenth century, the poems of Ephraem against Julian have still to take their proper place in modern historical assessments of this ruler.

If the reign of Julian comes into sharper focus when the mass of literary evidence is reduced to its principal components and the merits of the various reports are judiciously assessed, further control and clarification can still be had from the non-literary evidence. In this category we may include the numerous dated edicts of Julian in the Theodosian Code.[14] Written in a crabbed and at times almost impenetrable Latin, these documents are a sure guide to the evolution of the emperor's policies and the calculated caution with which he enunciated them. They take the historian immediately into the world of daily administration and show Julian at work in a way unknown to the rhetoric of eulogy or invective. The formal edicts are a particularly useful control on the frequently less disciplined remarks of the emperor in his literary works. It is a rare privilege for the ancient historian to be able to compare from original materials the public and the private worlds of a head of state.

The coinage of Julian is another valuable control over the literature. It is a complex coinage, which still awaits the full-scale treatment it deserves.[15] Yet even with uncertainties of chronology

---

[12] The invectives have been published with German translation by E. Beck, *Corpus Scriptorum Christianorum Orientalium* 174–5, Scriptores Syri 78–9 (1957).

[13] See below, p. 104 and plate at p. 111.

[14] These are conveniently included in J. Bidez and F. Cumont, *Iuliani Epistulae Leges Poematia Fragmenta Varia* (1922).

[15] Cf. J. P. C. Kent, *Numismatic Chronicle* 19 (1959), 109 ff.

and interpretation, the coins from the west and east of the empire furnish a clear view of Julian's ascendancy, claims, and aspirations. In some issues, such as the re-appearance of Julian's philosophic beard, the numismatists have paid insufficient attention to the texts,[16] so that the juxtaposition of literature and coins can be as fruitful for numismatics as for history. We have already implied that no numismatist has ever noticed Ephraem's lines on the bull coinage.

In their portraits of the emperor the coins, like the statues which survive, give an impression of appearance and personality which is relevant to an understanding of the reign. The look of Julian was the subject of many a jest in his lifetime and the occasion of a savage portrait by Gregory. The flamboyant manner in which Julian himself treats the matter shows that he was sensitive about it. Official representations have accordingly no small interest. The international image of the emperor is at issue.

Finally in the category of non-literary evidence are the inscriptions. As often, these keep—as visibly as when they were cut—the claims and aspirations of a historical moment that lasted only a short time. They proclaim certainties that were in fact nothing but hopes or ideals: freedom or a new order of the ages. The epigraphic texts reflect the religious struggles of Julian's age and the subtle ways in which the language of Christianity was converted to the service of revived paganism. From a few of the more elaborate inscriptions we can deduce the achievements in which Julian took his greatest pride, those which he wanted proclaimed throughout his world.

It was because of the equal ardour of his friends and his enemies that a figure as amply documented as Julian became in a relatively short span of time encrusted with legend. To reach the historical emperor as he reigned in succession to Constantius II from A.D. 361 to 363, to comprehend how he arrived at so great an eminence from a scholarly seclusion, the historian must listen above all to the authentic, contemporary voices. He must even try to hear them when they are almost inaudibly reproduced in a later age.

[16] See below, p. 61, n. 13.

CHAPTER TWO

The Personality of the Emperor

WHAT sort of a person was Julian? It is reasonable to establish, where possible, those traits of character which may explain the actions and decisions of a monarch. When Julian was dead, Gregory of Nazianzus asserted that the appearance of the young man he had known at Athens presaged even then the reign that was to follow.[1] Gregory was observant, but perhaps any school-boy would have watched with particular attention a nephew of Constantine the Great and a cousin of the reigning emperor, Constantius II.

It seemed to Gregory that no good would come of that flabby and disjointed neck, those quivering shoulders, those darting eyes with their wild gaze, those unsteady feet. He marked the scorn which Julian breathed through his conspicuous nose, his nervous and uncontrolled laughter, his irrational nodding and bobbing about. Julian's speech was staccato, his questions confused and his answers no better. This is not a friendly portrait, but the accuracy of its outlines is not in doubt. A sycophant like the consul Mamertinus singled out some of the same features for more flattering treatment. The emperor's strong neck often ran with sweat under the strain of ceaseless toil. His eyes glittered with astral fires (*sidereis ignibus*).[2] Similarly Ammianus, another admirer, described the flashing eyes, the thick neck, the straight nose, and the broad shoulders.[3] He adds that Julian was short of stature and hirsute.

---

[1] Greg. Naz., *orat.* 5.23 (Migne *PG* 35.692B).
[2] Mamertinus, *Panegyr.* 6.4. The speech is included in Sir Roger Mynors, *Panegyrici Latini XII* (Oxford Classical Texts). Cf. G. Barabino, *Claudio Mamertino: Il Panegirico dell' Imperatore Giuliano* (1965).   [3] Amm. Marc. 25.4.22.

The descriptions complement one another, and they are illustrated adequately by the numismatic and sculpted portraits. We can see the long and straight nose, with its supercilious aspect, and the large neck. It takes only a little imagination to revive the fires of those intense eyes. The details of nervous behaviour—constant bodily motion, undisciplined laughter, abrupt speech—are not in themselves implausible. Although the partisans of Julian did not, for obvious reasons, record such characteristics, they perhaps help to interpret the abusive label pinned on Julian by some of his discontented soldiers in Gaul—a talking mole (*loquax talpa*).[4] Short, hairy, agitated, and talkative, Julian must have recognized to his discomfort that the expression was cruelly appropriate.

It is in fact Julian himself who provides confirmation of Gregory's allegations of nervous intensity. When the people of Antioch taunted the emperor toward the end of his life with attacks on his beard, he replied in a work full of sarcasm and ironic self-disparagement. The *Misopogon* (Beard-Hater) is a work which might have been witty, but the bitterness of its angry and sensitive author overwhelmed his efforts at humour. Because his face was not handsome by nature, he sought to punish it, he said, by adding a beard. He wore his chin as goats do: Julian could not have forgotten that those soldiers in Gaul had also once called him a goat, not a man (*capella, non homo*).[5] Furthermore, as Julian warmed to his bitter irony, he declared that he seldom cut his hair or nails, 'and if you would like to learn something that is usually a secret, my chest is shaggy and covered with hair, like the breasts of lions who are kings among beasts'.[6] Julian's unsettling laughter can be heard throughout the *Misopogon*.

Somehow Julian's success had turned sour by then, and in the attempt to protest and to justify his life he gave much of himself away. He looked back nostalgically to the years of his military service in Gaul. The boorish Celts more easily put up with his character; they loved him, he said, because their character was like his. They appreciated him. As for the Antiochenes, 'Why, in the

---

[4] Amm. Marc. 17.11.1.   [5] Amm. Marc. 17.11.1.   [6] Julian, *Misop.* 339B.

name of the gods, are you ungrateful to me?'⁷ This petulant and self-righteous cry is a clue to Julian's character.

He was a man of ostentatious simplicity. Julian boasted of his asceticism in response to the Antiochenes' charges of boorish and uncivilized behaviour: 'Sleepless nights on straw and a diet that is anything but filling make my character austere and an enemy to a luxurious city.'⁸ As a philosopher transformed in Gaul into a soldier, Julian repudiated luxury and disciplined himself beyond the capabilities of most men. His way of life was indeed abnormal and required justification. In his panegyric Mamertinus tried to explain that the self-denying and strict regimen which Julian imposed upon himself was not meant to provide a model for his subjects. Rather he lived austerely to make life delightful for others.⁹ The Antiochenes would certainly not have agreed.

Libanius attempted on several occasions to justify Julian's behaviour to his fellow-citizens. As the emperor entered upon his fourth consulate on 1 January 363, Libanius undertook the duties of eulogy which Mamertinus had discharged at Constantinople exactly a year earlier. 'Your appetites are controlled and the power of sleep has been overcome', proclaimed the sophist. He knew that Julian had been criticized for his asceticism: 'In fact, because of this armour of self-control, he may perhaps even lose the praise it deserves, since the very impossibility of a life ordered on these lines falling under the spell of ignoble passions detracts from the feeling of admiration.'¹⁰ After Julian's death, Libanius, in his elaborate Funeral Oration, dilated on his hero's frugality, abstemiousness, and superhuman capacity for work. He also adverted to the emperor's total disinterest in sex.¹¹ According to Libanius, Julian was naturally inclined to continence.

Ammianus observed that if Julian's detractors had been able to uncover evidence of sexual liaisons they would undoubtedly have made them known.¹² The abstinence of Julian was universally acknowledged by friend and foe alike, and it is an important

---

⁷ Julian, *Misop.* 370C. ⁸ Julian, *Misop.* 340B.
⁹ Mamertinus, *Panegyr.* 12.2. ¹⁰ Libanius, *orat.* 12.94–5.
¹¹ Libanius, *orat.* 18.179. ¹² Amm. Marc. 25.4.3.

feature of the austerity of Julian's life. At the time he was appointed Caesar by Constantius in November 355, he was given Constantius' sister Helena as a wife in what was manifestly a political union. A child was engendered, but both mother and offspring perished in childbirth. Had it not been for that single encounter, in the opinion of Libanius, Julian 'would have ended his days knowing nothing of human sexual intercourse save by report'. It seems clear that Julian had no emotional attachment to Helena. He himself declared that he had never written her a letter which he would not gladly have had read by the entire world.[13] Some malicious tongues even alleged that he had engineered her death.

In the asceticism so integral to his character, Julian was markedly different from the two men of the ancient past whom he most revered. Writing to Themistius, he referred to his old and intimidating desire to rival Alexander the Great and Marcus Aurelius,[14] the former distinguished for his courage and the latter for his virtue. Julian's view of Alexander and Marcus comes through most clearly in his satirical dialogue, *The Caesars*, in which both appear conspicuously. Neither lays claim to an austere life like Julian's, but their virtues cast light on those which Julian sought in himself. Alexander subdued the Persians in the name of Hellenism and forced the conquered peoples to recognize his valour. It was precisely during his preparations for a great campaign against Persia that Julian wrote the speech of Alexander in his *Caesars*. And Marcus was presented as the winner of the competition in that satire—a humble and upright ruler who openly and repeatedly confessed his error in entrusting the empire to Commodus, his own son. Julian must have had this mistake in mind when he rejected the pleas of courtiers to remarry and produce a son to succeed him. According to Libanius, 'he replied that that was the very thing that deterred him, lest his children, if degenerate, should be legal heirs to the throne and bring ruin on

---

[13] Julian, *Lettres*, ed. Bidez (2nd edition, 1960), no. 80, p. 89; cf. Libanius, *orat.* 18.179.
[14] Julian, *To Themistius* 253A.

themselves'.[15] So a natural disinclination to approach another
woman found its justification in the error of the admirable Marcus.

Alexander, as he appeared in the *Caesars*, had also made his
mistakes: 'If some things I did seemed cruel, I never was so to the
innocent, but only to those who had often and in many ways
thwarted me . . . , and even my offences against these, which were
due to the emergency of the time, were followed by remorse
(*metameleia*).'[16] Here Julian is using one of his old heroes to
justify himself, for even Ammianus had to fault him in the matter
of cruelty toward those who had stood in Julian's way. Once a
man has chosen his heroes, it is remarkable how efficiently they
are cast in his likeness. Neither Alexander nor Marcus really bore
any great resemblance to Julian.

In the *Caesars* both Julian's heroes assert that they sought to
follow the gods. Alexander said of Heracles, 'I admired and followed him, so far as a mere man may follow in the footsteps of a
god.' Marcus, when asked the noblest ambition in life, replied
modestly, 'To imitate the gods'; and when questioned as to why he
ate bread and drank wine instead of ambrosia and nectar, he confessed that he perhaps erred in 'nourishing his body as he did'.[17]
That was another point in favour of the author of *The Caesars*.
But closeness to gods, avowed and felt, was supremely important
in Julian's view of Alexander and Marcus, and in his perception
of himself. He had always felt close to divine forces. 'For all that
I feel awe of the gods,' he wrote, 'I love, I revere, I venerate them
and in short have precisely the same feelings toward them as one
would have towards kind masters or teachers or fathers or
guardians or any beings of that sort.'[18]

Julian was highly susceptible to religious experiences of a
mystical kind. He was by no means alone in this enthusiasm, as
the popularity of the Neo-Platonist teachers in the fourth century
makes plain. There is no reason to doubt the genuineness of
Julian's fanaticism or of the supernatural concomitants of it.

[15] Libanius, *orat.* 18.181.   [16] Julian, *Caesars* 325B.
[17] Julian, *Caesars* 325A (Alexander and Heracles); 333C–D (Marcus).
[18] Julian, 212B.

When Julian heard of a teacher who was said to make a statue of Hecate smile and laugh, and to make the torches in her hand burst into flame, he is reported by Eunapius to have declared that he had discovered the man he was seeking.[19] In the long myth with which Julian concluded his address to the Cynic Heracleius, he outlined in scarcely veiled terms his intimate relationship to the gods, especially Zeus, Helios, Athene, and Hermes. To them he ascribed the course of his career. The youth who is patently Julian in the myth declares to his gods, 'Do with me what you will', and Helios replies to him, 'We are your benefactors and friends and saviours... We will be with you everywhere.'[20] Julian believed that they were, and he acted accordingly. Like most religious enthusiasts, he was always capable of seeing divine intervention in the affairs of men, even when his own volition was involved. When the troops at Paris in 360 were shouting that he was now Augustus, Julian retreated to pray. He asked Zeus for a sign and received one. He was not to oppose the will of the army. Words like hypocrisy or dishonesty cannot easily be invoked in the case of a personality in which ambition is so inextricably linked to religiosity.

Dreams and visions were important to Julian, and he experienced them at decisive moments in his life. He was more rather than less typical of ancient men in his predisposition to such psychic phenomena and in his credulity. While in Gaul and still at the rank of Caesar, Julian wrote in a letter that he had had a prophetic dream in which he saw a very tall tree bending over to the ground from its own weight and height, and beside it a small shoot in flower growing out of the roots of the great tree. He feared for the safety of the young plant and when he drew nearer he saw the great tree falling to the ground. The small tree was still standing; its roots remained in the earth, and an unknown person advised the dreamer not to fear for its safety. 'God knows what this means,' wrote Julian.[21] For the young cousin of the reigning monarch, ambition was rising. The two appearances of

---

[19] Eunapius, *Lives of the Sophists* p. 475. [20] Julian 232D; 233D.
[21] Julian, *Lettres* (Bidez), no. 14, p. 21.

the *genius publicus* in nocturnal visions, as recorded by Ammianus —once to encourage the new Augustus and again to signal his approaching demise—seem so neatly coherent as to be legendary, but they are not misleading in what they imply about Julian himself.

The emperor's spiritual life equipped him to dissemble with confidence. He grew accustomed to saying and to practising what he did not believe. For ten years he comported himself publicly as a Christian while worshipping the pagan gods.[22] Libanius goes out of his way to excuse this behaviour on the reasonable grounds of prudence. The same excuse may also be advanced in extenuation of the two fulsome panegyrics of Constantius which Julian composed in Gaul. While the second of these may possibly contain a few oblique hints at the rupture between the two men,[23] the two discourses nevertheless give an impression of unstinting admiration which not even political necessity nor rhetorical theory can free from the charge of sycophancy. Julian's true hatred of his cousin was first made public in his letter to the Athenians in 361 (and presumably in his letters, now lost, to other cities too), and yet this confession was also due to necessity since Julian was under compulsion to explain why he was launching a civil war. Constantius was not yet dead. A little while later, when he was, Julian gave full honours to the deceased monarch. He attended his funeral, and Mamertinus a few weeks later spoke of him as deified (*divus*), an epithet the early Christian emperors were by no means averse to bestowing upon their predecessors.

With dissembling for reasons of prudence, Julian conjoined an impatience and an intolerance that constituted another aspect of the irrational side of his character. The whole of the *Misopogon* sprang from these emotions. The end of the *Caesars* displays Julian's pent-up fury against his uncle Constantine in combination with his intolerance of the Christians and his aversion to sex. Pleasure dresses up Constantine and leads him off to Incontinence,

---

[22] Julian, *Lettres* (Bidez), no. III [434 D], p. 191.
[23] See below, pp. 43–4.

with whom Jesus is cohabiting.[24] Already in Gaul Julian had revealed his temper to his friends. Intolerant of Constantius' men, whom he denounced as an 'accursed band of labourers' and 'bandits',[25] Julian said he would feel no pain if Constantius were to remove him from his position. When the Cynic Heracleius made bold, once Julian was emperor, to attack him in the traditional Cynic manner (something Constantius had managed to tolerate with equanimity), the new emperor composed an elaborate reply in which the poor Cynic was presented as not really knowing his business. Heracleius had compared Julian with the goat-like Pan. The shaft had struck home. For certain periods Julian seemed able to contain the irascible and intemperate side of his nature, but it was always there. Libanius had no difficulty in filling up a whole speech with warnings to the Antiochenes on the possible consequences of the emperor's anger.

It is not surprising that a man of such a complex nervous temperament, superstitious and calculating, easily wounded in his pride, should have had few friends. Even his relationship with Libanius, which rested upon the solid rock of pagan Hellenism, was not wholly untroubled. A small group of intellectuals, of whom the principals were the physician Oribasius and the Neo-Platonist mystics Maximus and Priscus, constituted Julian's intimates. These men stood by him to the end. A remarkable mosaic at Syrian Apamea, in which Socrates and his disciples are depicted, has been connected with a Neo-Platonic attack on Christian iconography under Julian, whereby Socrates has replaced Jesus and the representation of Socrates suggests Julian himself.[26] But even if current propaganda strove to present the emperor as a philosophic master amid his followers, there is no indication that he actually played such a role.[27]

[24] Julian, *Caesars* 336 A.

[25] Julian, *Lettres* (Bidez), no. 14 [385B–C], p. 22: *Kleptai* and *theomīses ergastērion*.

[26] J. and J. Ch. Balty, *Dialogues d'histoire ancienne 1974 = Annales littéraires de l'université de Besançon* 166 (1974), 270–6; cf. n. 128 *bis* and plate VIII. It has long been noticed that Julian's death-bed scene in Ammianus, Book 25, is reminiscent of the death of Socrates.

[27] R. T. Wallis, *Neoplatonism* (1972), p. 96: 'Several letters and theological

Julian clearly believed in his own destiny. His courage and fortitude were not illusory. His nearness to his gods strengthened his conviction; and his austere style of life, with its isolation from normal human contacts, equipped him for the single-minded pursuit of his goals. He can easily take his place in the class of ascetic revolutionaries, which included in later times such other isolated and self-denying activists as Lenin and Mao-Tse-Tung.[28] Like them, Julian was neither gregarious nor, in the social sense of the term, even civilized, as the Antiochenes were only too well aware. As a true ascetic revolutionary, he avoided emotional or sexual entanglements, although he was not free from anger. His life became consecrated to his career as a pagan emperor. His inspiration and motivation came from no mortal source, for between himself and his gods there was no room for the ordinary ties of humanity. In such a personality the plans devised by cold calculation served to turn dreams and visions into reality.

---

essays survive by Julian himself; their philosophy is largely a popularization of Iamblichus' teaching, as is that of the attractive little "pagan catechism" by Julian's praetorian prefect Sallustius [*sic*] preserved under the title "On the Gods and the World".' On the identity of Sallustius, or rather Salutius, see Appendix III below. The intricacies of Neo-Platonic thought are lucidly disentangled in Wallis' book.

[28] Cf. Bruce Mazlish, *The Revolutionary Ascetic* (1976). I cannot accept the main points of his analysis. He seems unaware of any ascetic revolutionaries before the seventeenth century.

CHAPTER THREE

The Heritage of Adolescence

WHILE none of our knowledge of Julian's youth derives from documents of the time, the rich contemporary evidence for his mature years sheds much light on what went before. The significance of Julian's experiences in the twenty-four years that preceded his designation as Caesar in 355 can scarcely be exaggerated, for he was a member of the house of Constantine and therefore exposed to all the tensions and dangers of royalty under the rule of another branch of the family.

Julian's father, Julius Constantius, had been a half-brother of Constantine the Great. While the two brothers were both the offspring of Constantius I (sometimes called Chlorus), one of the founders of the fourth-century dynasty, only Constantine was born of the barmaid Helena; and Constantine's mother did not look favourably upon the three sons of her husband by a second marriage, as well as their progeny and their relatives. Yet it seemed that Constantine in his last years had freed himself to some degree from Helena's prejudices. In 333 one half-brother, Flavius Delmatius, was consul, and in about 335 Constantine began to entrust two sons of Delmatius as well as Julius Constantius himself with responsible or honorific positions in the empire. Hannibalianus, a son of Delmatius, was given authority over Armenia, and another son, also called Delmatius, over Illyricum; Julius Constantius, Julian's father, was honoured with the consulate of 335. A few years before this happened Julius Constantius' second wife, a lady from an affluent Bithynian family, had been delivered at Constantinople of the infant Julian and, not many months later, died.

The exact date of Julian's birth has long been a matter of scholarly controversy. If we cannot be absolutely certain that the year was 331, nevertheless that is the most reasonable hypothesis on the basis of the divergent indications of antiquity.[1] The month and day cannot be determined: 6 November, sometimes affirmed, is only a doublet for the day on which Julian became Caesar, and May or June are due to the ignorance of a scholiast. In any case, the boy passed his tenderest years in Constantine's new capital, for which he always felt a special affection; and although deprived of a mother's care, he must have shared in the growing spirit of confidence that Constantine's hostility toward the children of the second wife of Constantius I was changing to benignity and preferment. Julian was being raised a Christian, as befitted the nephew of the first Christian emperor.

Hope and optimism were, however, suddenly and brutally extinguished by the death of Constantine on 22 May 337. The disposition of imperial authority which he had made in the final years had given every sign of reconciling his own three children with his half-brother and nephews by assigning all six a share in the power. Although such an arrangement could be paralleled in the aftermath of Diocletian's resignation, when six men briefly ruled the empire, there were those who frowned upon it— perhaps recalling the failures of the earlier experiment and perhaps reflecting that power too generously divided is no power at all. The army declared that it would accept as joint emperors only the three sons of Constantine,[2] and we may readily appreciate that they acquiesced in this. They may, indeed, have encouraged the army in its position. Certainly, considerable confusion and instability dominated the summer of 337. It was not until 9

---

[1] For a recent review of the problems, see G. W. Bowersock, *Gibbon et Rome* (1977), pp. 203–4. R. Browning, *The Emperor Julian* (1975), p. 32, follows the *Prosopography of the Later Roman Empire* (1971), p. 477, in reviving without new evidence the old birth-date of 332. Neither mentions the powerful arguments for rejecting it in N. H. Baynes, *Journal of Hellenic Studies* 45 (1925), 252. The date of 331 appears in J. Bidez, *La vie de l'empereur Julien* (1930), p. 10 and in the introduction by A. F. Norman to the Loeb Libanius, vol. 1 (1969), p. ix.

[2] Eusebius, *Life of Constantine* 68.

1. Gold coin of Constantius II, with reverse (*Gloria rei publicae*) also used by Julian. Mint of Rome.

2. Silver coin of Julian in Gaul. Mint of Lyon.

September that the new *Augusti* were proclaimed, and they were the sons of Constantine with no others.

A strange document was said to have been extorted from the hand of Constantine's corpse. It was alleged to contain a change of mind about Julius Constantius and his nephews, and this was used to justify their exclusion from the list of *Augusti*. Whatever the truth of that story, the fortunes of Julian's family were quickly altered. Either before or very soon after 9 September his father and eight of his relatives were murdered. Only Julian and his own half-brother Gallus were spared. Their extreme youth appears to have been their salvation. The massacre was a stunning blow, eliminating at once the chief rivals of the sons of Constantine. Of the three new *Augusti* Constantius II survived the longest, outlasting his elder and his younger brothers. He was Julian's immediate predecessor as emperor and the man Julian held personally responsible for the extermination of his family.

While Constantius denied that he had ordered the murders, it is as hard for modern historians as it was for Julian not to suspect him. The savagery of what happened, in a Christian court, had a scaring effect on the six year old boy: twenty-four years later he counted the toll of victims in his letter to the Athenians when he moved to face Constantius in civil war, and Libanius marked the murders as the major event of Julian's infancy. Motherless from birth, Julian now became fatherless as well. He was sent out of Constantinople and turned over to the gentle ministrations of his maternal grandmother in Bithynia.

For several years Julian's education, and presumably his brother's, was in the hands of Eusebius, the Arian bishop of Nicomedia, whose attention to the young princes may well have helped to ensure their survival.[3] We may be certain that Eusebius laboured to improve the Christian knowledge of his pupils, but for Julian another of his teachers at this time had a far more profound impact. In the *Misopogon* the emperor paid a luminous tribute to Mardonius, a Scythian eunuch who had been brought up in the house of his grandfather to be a tutor to Julian's mother.[4]

---

[3] Amm. Marc. 22.9.4.   [4] Julian, *Misop.* 352A–354A.

According to Julian, from the completion of his seventh year, thus from 338, Mardonius instructed him in the pagan classics, especially Homer and Hesiod. Libanius described this teacher as the admirable eunuch who guarded the youth's virtue.[5] In bidding farewell some years later to his valued Neo-Platonist counsellor, Salutius, in Gaul, Julian affectingly evoked the emotions he had felt when finally compelled to take leave of Mardonius. 'I felt the same anguish as when at home I first left my tutor. For everything flashed across my mind at once: the labours that we shared and endured together, our unfeigned and candid conversations, our innocent and upright association, our cooperation in all that was good . . . How alike were our ways! How precious our friendship!'[6]

It is not known whether Mardonius was a Christian or pagan, but it is unlikely he would have been taken into Basilina's home as a tutor had he not been a Christian. His exposition of Homer and the other classics, together with a personality to which the orphaned Julian clearly warmed, provided the foundation for his pupil's knowledge of classical Hellenism. Since personal attachments were so rare in Julian's life and were formed with such difficulty, it may not be rash to see in the few friendships of his maturity—exclusively with teachers, be they sophists, physicians, or philosophers—an attempt to find another Mardonius.

In the interstices of his education Julian spent time on his grandmother's estate only a few kilometres from the shore of the Sea of Marmara. Writing from Gaul some fifteen years later, Julian could still recall the happiness he knew in the calm and beauty of that place. There was no merchant or sailor to be a nuisance, and yet by going up on a little hill one could see the sea, the ships, the islands, and on the other side Constantinople. One was far enough from the water's edge not to find the refuse it washed up, but instead there were only the flowers and perfumed vegetation. 'When I was quite young this spot seemed best of all . . . Now that I am a man I long for that old way of life.'[7] Like the teaching

[5] Libanius, *orat.* 18.11.   [6] Julian 241C.
[7] Julian, *Lettres* (Bidez) no. 4 [427B–C], p. 13.

of Mardonius, the peace of that estate was an irretrievable loss.

The idyll into which the massacre of his family had plunged Julian was soon broken off, at the onset of adolescence. It is possible that Julian had already been compelled to leave Bithynia about 340 when the bishop Eusebius was translated to the see of Constantinople. A hint in Libanius implies that Mardonius went with him to the capital at that time.[8] But more unsettling to the young man was the exile which Constantius imposed upon him and his brother in 342.[9] The emperor must have viewed with increasing concern the growth to manhood of these two princes of the blood. He may have reckoned that a protracted season of guarded isolation would both keep them out of harm's way and render their character anodyne for the future. If so, he was badly mistaken.

Julian and Gallus were interned on the royal estate called Macellum (which simply means 'the enclosure') in Cappadocia. The place was agreeably situated near the foot of Mount Argaeus not far from Caesarea, the modern Kayseri in Turkey.[10] There was a splendid palace, surrounded by gardens; but for all this it was a place of exile. The two boys spent six years at Macellum, and for Julian this was the formative period from his twelfth to his eighteenth year. As Julian later wrote to the Athenians, no one of his own age was ever allowed to come near him. 'We were watched as though we were in some Persian garrison, since no stranger came to see us and not one of our old friends was allowed to visit us. We lived shut off from all serious learning and from all free intercourse, in a glittering servitude and sharing the exercises of our slaves as if they were our comrades.'[11] According to Eunapius, royal eunuchs made it their business to keep vigilant watch over the Christian faith of their two charges.[12]

[8] Libanius, *orat.* 18.11. On this cf. N. H. Baynes, op. cit. (n. 1), 252.

[9] For the date, established by Baynes and followed by Bidez, see A. F. Norman, *Libanius*, Loeb vol. 1 (1969), p. ix note a. Browning, op. cit. (n. 1), p. 42 follows an old and discredited chronology which dates the exile from 344, and he is therefore forced to keep Libanius in Nicomedia a year after he is now known to have left it (Browning, p. 52).

[10] Amm. Marc. 15.2.7. Sozomen 5.2 (Migne, *PG* 67.1213B).

[11] Julian 271C.   [12] Eunapius, *Lives of the Sophists* p. 473.

It is by no means easy to learn the details of this crucial exile. Once Constantius was buried and Julian's public attitude toward his predecessor became more moderate than it had been in the letter to the Athenians, he spoke only rarely of the years in Cappadocia. His eulogists, like Mamertinus and Libanius, shied away altogether from the humiliation of that period. Even in the elaborate biographical narrative which comprises most of Libanius' funeral oration for Julian, the six years at Macellum are totally suppressed. This lack of candour caused serious confusion in the later tradition, for the church historian Socrates, writing with Libanius' account before him, inevitably confused the facts of Julian's education concerning the time before and the time after the exile. Fortunately Sozomen, working from Socrates but with the aid of additional sources, managed to import some clarification into the narrative.

Those six lonely years of Julian's early and middle adolescence were not wasted. Mardonius had cultivated the love of books in him, and Julian carried on at Macellum the voracious reading he had started under Mardonius' inspiration. Constantius had cut off the princes from everything but books, and for Julian that made all the difference. He embarrassed the royal eunuchs, for, as Eunapius said, 'He had their books so thoroughly by heart that they fretted at the scantiness of their erudition.'[13] These will have been Christian texts. But Julian had access to the pagan classics as well. In a revealing letter written to Ecdicius, the prefect of Egypt, after the Arian bishop, George of Cappadocia, was killed in a riot at Alexandria, Julian asked that part of the library of George be salvaged. He knew what the library contained because he had been permitted to work through most of it when he had been at Macellum and George was still in Cappadocia. There were many works of philosophy and rhetoric, as well as Christian texts. 'I know the books of George', wrote Julian, 'if not all of them, at any rate most.'[14] The pagan classics in George's library were those he asked Ecdicius to confiscate at that time

[13] ibid., loc. cit.
[14] Julian, *Lettres* (Bidez), no. 107 [378c], p. 185.

some fifteen years or more after he had read them. They had obviously made an impression.

Only once did Constantius himself go to Macellum during the residence of Julian and Gallus. That visit was the first occasion on which the emperor saw Julian face to face. The remoteness of Constantius in his court of sycophants had ensured that he never actually confronted the prince he thought might one day threaten him. In 348 the long years of exile came to an end. Perhaps the boys were judged safe. At any rate we can be certain that the eunuchs found themselves unable to teach Julian anything more, so that he was restored to the schools of Constantinople upon his return from Cappadocia. His older half-brother, released at the same time, merely continued his life as a prisoner—but at the court instead of at Macellum.

Julian, replete with six years' reading and in his eighteenth year, became a pupil of Nicocles and Hecebolius. The former, a pagan rival of Libanius, and the latter, a Christian whose faith was readily shaken when Julian became emperor, undertook to train him in the branches of rhetoric. But Constantius soon had him transferred yet again. Now on the threshold of manhood (*pro sēbos*), as Libanius wrote later, he showed his princely nature. 'This allowed Constantius no rest, and so, fearful that his capital, which was so influential in the formulation of public opinion and in matters of government the peer of Rome, should be attracted to the young man's excellence, with some untoward consequences for himself, he had him packed off to Nicomedia, since that city would cause him not nearly so much alarm, and there he provided facilities for his education.'[15]

Libanius had been teaching in Nicomedia since 344, when a cabal of rival colleagues, including Nicocles, had had him driven out of Constantinople.[16] When Julian arrived in Nicomedia in late 348 or in 349, he had been forced by Hecebolius to swear that he would not attend Libanius' lectures. It appears that Julian

---

[15] Libanius, *orat.* 18.13.
[16] Cf. P. Petit, *Libanius et la vie municipale à Antioche* (1955), p. xx. For what follows in the text, cf. Baynes, op. cit. (n. 1).

suffered more from the animosities of an academic clique at Constantinople than from any concern for the preservation of his Christian principles. At Nicomedia the young man dutifully adhered to the letter of his oath, but he hired someone at great expense to copy down Libanius' lectures for him. He thus became the great sophist's spiritual disciple and felt free, when he was serving in Gaul some years later, to send Libanius copies of the panegyrics he was then composing. This indirect tutelage cannot have lasted very long. By the end of 349 Libanius had returned in triumph, at the summons of the emperor, to resume his teaching in Constantinople—where he remained for about four years before returning to his native Antioch.

While Julian was studying at Nicomedia, his half-brother Gallus was elevated, in 351, to the rank of Caesar to share with Constantius the burdens of empire. Uprisings and pretenders in the West were diverting the emperor's energies to that quarter, leaving the eastern flank exposed to Persian hostility. Constantius needed someone to represent him there, and with both his brothers now dead he turned of necessity to Gallus. Julian's unremitting study took him about this time to the masters of Neo-Platonic philosophy in western Asia Minor.

He passed first to Pergamum. There he sat at the feet of the aged Aedesius, who taught the interpretation of Plato which had taken its origins in the previous century from the mystical writings of Plotinus and Porphyry. Porphyry's influential disciple Iamblichus of Syrian Chalcis had been Aedesius' own teacher, and thus by attaching himself to Aedesius Julian placed himself in the direct line of Neo-Platonic philosophers. While at Pergamum, he listened to two of Aedesius' eminent pupils, Eusebius and Chrysanthius. Their disagreements exposed him to the varieties of Neo-Platonism in respect to the working of wonders and the emphasis upon supernatural experience. It was Iamblichus who had been the first Neo-Platonist to prefer magic and ritual to reason. Julian likewise preferred the miraculous to the logical strain of this late Platonism.[17] He was, now as he

[17] Eunapius, *Lives of the Sophists* pp. 474–5. Cf. E. R. Dodds, *Journal of*

approached the age of twenty, not only very literate but, in his loneliness, very impressionable.

Aedesius' pupil, Eusebius, described to Julian the erudition and eloquence of another of Aedesius' protégés, Maximus of Ephesus, but he deplored Maximus' scorn of logical demonstration. He compared the wonders wrought by Maximus, the theurgy or—in plain language—magic, to the work of a madman. It was from Eusebius that Julian heard about the laughing statue of Hecate and the torches that automatically burst into flame, all under the power of Maximus. Eusebius counselled Julian to avoid the 'stagey miracle-worker' and to attach the greatest importance to a spiritual purification attained by reason. But Julian would have none of his advice and departed immediately to go to Maximus. So Eunapius says, and it is certain that at this time he did indeed go to Maximus. He was a willing disciple. Julian himself dated his conversion to paganism from the year 351, and Libanius paid tribute to the role of Maximus. In his address to Julian on 1 January 363, he makes it plain that it was under the influence of Maximus that Julian cast off his Christian beliefs and embraced the gods of paganism. Echoing the propaganda of Julian's reign, Libanius declared that Julian's conversion was the beginning of freedom for the world.[18] No youth could have been more ripe for conversion than Julian in 351.

The commitment he made then was deep and lasting. It brought him still closer to the pagan authors he knew so well, and it put a chasm between him and the detested Constantius. The theurgy of Maximus soon made him crave the theurgy of Priscus, another of Aedesius' pupils who was less addicted to logic than Eusebius. Priscus he found a few years later at Athens, and it was to him he wrote subsequently from Gaul in the hope of acquiring the writings of Iamblichus on the sacred text of the Neo-Platonic

---

Roman Studies 37 (1967), 59: 'It would seem that even in the generation after Iamblichus theurgy was not yet fully accepted in the Neoplatonic school.' Dodds' article entitled 'Theurgy and its Relation to Neoplatonism' was reprinted as an appendix in his *Greeks and the Irrational* (1956) and is still invaluable on this subject.

[18] Libanius, *orat.* 12.34. Cf. *orat.* 13.12.

theurgists, the Chaldaean Oracles.[19] Julian's appetite for all this was insatiable and explains the presence of Priscus and Maximus not only in his court but on the Persian campaign and by his death-bed east of the Tigris.

For ten years Julian concealed his new religion. He continued his public devotions in the Christian faith, although Libanius intimates that there were well-placed pagan intellectuals who knew of Julian's conversion and hoped for his future ascendance.[20] Through contacts in the cities of the Greek East they appear to have worked covertly toward this end. It was not so much that they were manipulating Julian. He counted himself one of them; he shared their aims. In the years immediately following the conversion Julian seemed genuinely to have had no ambition to supplant Constantius. After his studies in Ephesus with Maximus, Julian showed his single-mindedness by continuing his education at Athens. He was happy there, but the elimination of Gallus by Constantius only three years after he had been appointed Caesar not only warned Julian again of the many dangers at court but even for a while implicated him in them.

It was only the emperor's wife, Eusebia, who appears to have appreciated Julian in the court of Constantius, but she was a powerful advocate.[21] Thanks to her the suspicions which were levelled at him in the time of Gallus' removal and execution were dissipated. As Julian emerged into manhood, it was scarcely unexpected that the courtiers of Constantius, especially the

---

[19] Julian, *Lettres* (Bidez) no. 12, p. 19. On the Chaldaean Oracles, 'a collection of turgid and obscure hexameter oracles composed or collected during the reign of Marcus Aurelius': R. T. Wallis, *Neoplatonism* (1972), p. 105. Cf. H.Lewy, *Chaldaean Oracles and Theurgy* (1956). When Julian wrote Priscus to ask for Iamblichus' writings, he noted that a wonderful sign occurred as he was writing— presumably a twitch or spasm.

[20] Libanius, *orat* 13.13–14: 'You wept at the ruin of our temples . . . , and allowed those about you to observe in your present pain the aid to come. With the revival of such hopes, all the élite of intellect on continent and island aligned itself with you in good will, and united in preparing the throne for you, not by force of arms or point of sword but by hidden prayer and secret sacrifice.' See also *orat*. 14.42. Cf. P. Petit, op. cit. (n. 16), pp. 203 ff. on what A. F. Norman calls the 'pagan underground' in his Loeb annotations of the indicated passages of Libanius.

[21] Amm. Marc. 15.2.7; 15.8.3. Cf. Julian's panegyric in honour of Eusebia.

eunuch chamberlain who was yet another bearer of the name Eusebius, attempted to subvert any claim he might have to authority or influence. In his letter to Themistius Julian wrote eloquently of the dangers he experienced from his relatives and friends during the period of his study at Athens,[22]—a period which had been interrupted when Gallus died, by a summons to the emperor's court at Milan.

We may probably believe Julian's affirmation to the Athenians that he did not want the responsibility of the Caesarship which Constantius, at the instigation of Eusebia, thrust upon him in November of 355. He was devoted to his gods, to his teachers, and to his books. But that does not mean that he was indifferent to the fate of the empire or to his own role in determining it. Libanius stated that Julian was not interested at that time in the imperial purple but that he was eager for the restoration of pagan worship with its temples and sacrifices. Julian was prepared to take steps to bring that about, and there are oblique references in his letter to Themistius which suggest that he was already exerting himself for this purpose when he was still in Asia Minor: 'You are well aware of what I did, in the first place, in Ionia in opposition to one who was related to me by ties of blood, but even more closely by ties of friendship, and that on behalf of a foreigner with whom I was very slightly acquainted.'[23] In boasting of such treachery, Julian must be alluding to some support of a worthy pagan. Other acts of service which he mentions in the same passage are presumably to be explained in the same way.

The myth about Julian's own life at the conclusion of his address to the Cynic Heracleius similarly betrays a sense of destiny which could lead to intervention for the advancement of

[22] Julian 259B.

[23] Julian 259C. Julian's relations to Themistius, a great Athenian orator of his day, may be further illuminated by the document purportedly written by Themistius for Julian on how to rule. It survives only in an Arabic translation done from a Syriac version: J. Croissant, *Serta Leodiensia* (1930), 22 ff. Irfan Shahîd has prepared the text and translation for the Teubner *Themistius*, edited by G. Downey. The existence of the Arabic letter of Themistius lends support to the supposition that Julian's letter to the orator should certainly be dated after Julian became sole emperor.

the gods. If by 355 Julian did not envisage himself on his cousin's throne, he was nevertheless ready to join action with study. From the libraries of Constantinople, Nicomedia, and Cappadocia Julian had come to the smiling statues and blazing torches which gave new life to the classical Hellenism that had been the chief sustenance and companionship of his childhood. Now he wanted to change things somehow. The pupils of Aedesius recognized this and rejoiced.

CHAPTER FOUR

Gaul

THE frequency of barbarian invasions into Gaul gave increasing concern to Constantius and his counsellors in 355. The troubles were a legacy of the abortive attempt by Magnentius in 351 to supplant the emperor.[1] The popularity of this usurper in Gaul had been countered by an understanding between the emperor and the German tribes on the right bank of the Rhine. Magnentius was unable to survive an authorized migration of barbarian forces to the Gallic side of the river, and his cause was finished in 353. But the stability of the Rhine frontier was seriously undermined by Constantius' incautious deal. The Germans continued to push into Roman territory. A Frank by the name of Silvanus, when falsely charged with rebellion, ultimately decided that his safest course was actually to rebel; and when he did so in 355 Constantius was again forcefully reminded that all was not well in Gaul.

Julian's half-brother Gallus had been eliminated the previous year after being deposed from his position as Caesar at Antioch. Not even Julian, with all the hatred he displayed toward Constantius later in his letter to the Athenians, could conceal that Gallus' administration had been cruel and irregular. There was therefore some justification for the step Constantius took. If suspicion fell for a moment also upon Julian, it is evident that with the good will of the empress Eusebia it passed. When Constantius addressed himself to the problem of Gaul in the second half of 355, he was persuaded that he had again to appoint a

[1] On Magnentius, see the useful work of P. Bastien, *Le monnayage de Magnence* (1964).

royal representative. From Julian's panegyric to the empress, composed in the following year as well as from the account of Ammianus, we may believe that Eusebia encouraged Constantius in the choice of Julian. On 6 November Julian was named Caesar and suddenly found himself with an opportunity for action instead of contemplation.

Beginning with Julian's letter to the Athenians in 361 and continuing in the reports of Libanius, Eunapius, and Ammianus, the tradition about Constantius' dispatching the new Caesar to Gaul uniformly discredits the reigning emperor. It is alleged that Constantius wanted Julian to have no real power in Gaul. For the first two years of his service there Julian claimed that he was subordinate to the officers already in the Gallic provinces and was not even permitted to assemble troops.[2] He was watched, so he maintained, like the enemy and on the emperor's orders, lest he foment a revolt. Libanius said much the same in the Funeral Oration: 'he had authority for nothing save to wear the uniform'.[3] A similar claim reappears in Ammianus and can be inferred to have stood in the history of Eunapius, who in the *Lives of the Sophists* wrote that Constantius had not wanted Julian to rule in Gaul but to die there. As Julian wrote sarcastically to the Athenians, his principal task was to carry about the emperor's image and purple robe. In the winter of 355/6 he was sent into Gaul with a mere 360 soldiers, and by his account he was not able to accomplish much of anything in 356. Only with the fall from favour of one of the Gallic commanders in 357 was Julian finally placed in a position of authority—as he told the story in 361.

This melancholy version of Julian's first years in Gaul has been accorded far more credence than it deserves, presumably because Julian himself is the fundamental source for most of it. To be sure, Constantius and others might have felt some reasonable reservations about entrusting important military operations to a young man whose life had been largely confined to books and visions. But it can have been no secret that Julian was clever,

[2] Julian 277D–278B.   [3] Libanius, *orat.* 18.42.

3. Silver coin of Julian in Gaul. Mint of Arles.

4. Rare bronze coin of Julian (reverse: *Virtus exercitus Romanorum*).
Mint of Rome.

GAUL

Concordance of place-names

Arles: Arelate
Autun: Augustodunum
Auxerre: Autessiodurum
Cologne: Colonia Agrippina
Lyons: Lugdunum
Mainz: Moguntiacum
Paris: Lutetia
Sens: Agedincum
Strassburg: Argentoratum (Argentorate)
Trier: Augusta Treverorum
Vienne: Vienna (south of Lugdunum)
Zabern: Tabernae

THE FAMILY OF JULIAN

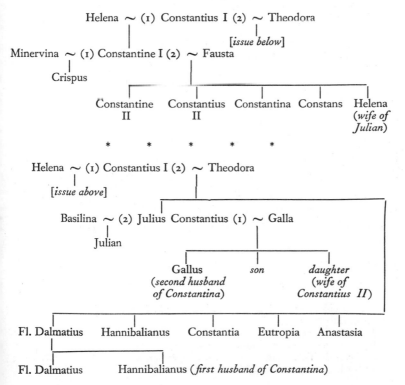

and Eusebia may not have been the only one to recognize that he was ready for a more active life. In preparation for his campaigns in Gaul Julian studied the Commentaries of Julius Caesar, which he took with him along with other edifying works (such as Plutarch's _Lives_) provided by the Empress herself.[4] A close examination of those early years in Gaul will show clearly that Julian and the others who followed him have substantially and deliberately misrepresented the circumstances of his career at that time and his relation with Constantius. Julian had full authority as Caesar, was glad of it, and used it.

Constantius went out with Julian for a certain distance as he sent him off to Gaul. The 360 soldiers were to accompany him on his journey. Obviously the main body of troops was stationed in the provinces already and awaited his arrival. As Julian was on his way the news came to him of the capture of Cologne by the Franks.[5] This was the site of an important Roman settlement at a strategic point on the Rhine, and its loss was not to be underestimated. Julian eventually recaptured Cologne, and the dating of this event is the essential piece in any accurate re-construction of the events of 355 to 357 in Gaul. For Julian succeeded in suggesting to the Athenians as well as to some modern historians who have read his communication that Cologne was not retaken until he gained military authority in 357. Ammianus knew better, for he places the event in 356. Julian himself inadvertently let the truth slip out when he observed that the barbarians had captured the colony ten months before he took it back.[6] Not all Julian's readers knew enough to read his remark with the knowledge that Cologne had fallen no later than November, 355. It was the late seventeenth-century Jansenist scholar Tillemont who spotted Julian's slip and realized—though the point has often been missed since—that Julian can be confuted out of his own mouth.[7]

---

[4] Julian 123D–124D, with echoes of Plutarch. Cf. _Lettres_ (Bidez) no. 26 [414C], p. 53 with Bidez's note 2.

[5] Amm. Marc. 15.8.19.

[6] Julian 279B (_pro mēnōn healōkuian pou deka_).

[7] Le Nain de Tillemont, _Histoire des Empereurs_, vol. 4 (1723), p. 683, note xxxvii: 'Cologne reprise par Julien en l'an 356.'

The recapture of Cologne in 356 is important not only because it tells something in itself about Julian's generalship but also because it is the end of a series of moves and military operations, all of which are therefore secured for 356.

After advancing to Vienne, south of Lyons, in the winter of 355/6, the new Caesar paused there until the advent of milder weather. Constantius' appointment of Julian was further publicized by the consulate he assigned him with himself as colleague for the year 356. On Julian's side the elaborate composition of a panegyric to the emperor, extolling his temperance and prudence, is vivid proof of the cordial relations which Julian was anxious to maintain with Constantius. The panegyric is a set piece, written according to the proper rhetorical principles; but its formal correctness does not absolve Julian of wilfully fostering the impression of dedication to the emperor and to Christianity. It would be wrong to conclude that Julian's policy toward Constantius at this time was necessarily calculating and Machiavellian. Julian was young and ambitious. He was glad of the opportunity he had been given, and he was scarcely in a position yet to repudiate the man who had given it to him. What was truly calculating was Julian's effort in 361 to persuade the Athenians that his relations with Constantius had been so different. In the panegyric of 356 Julian had even declared Constantius free of any guilt for misdeeds committed after the death of Constantine. This must have meant that Constantius was to feel no anxiety that Julian harboured resentment or bitterness over the massacre of his father and his relatives. Of course we know that he did.

In June of 356 Julian received word at Vienne that the veterans at Autun had been under attack by barbarians, who had made their way deep into Burgundy from the lands granted to them by Constantius on the left bank of the Rhine.[8] The walls of Autun were old and weak. After due deliberation and consultation with

[8] Reconstruction of the military history of Julian's years as Caesar depends largely upon the detailed narrative of Ammianus, who served in Gaul during the earlier part of Julian's command. Cf. I. Mueller-Seidl, *Historische Zeitschrift* 180 (1955), 225 ff. Julian himself says that he crossed the Rhine three times while still Caesar (280c).

those who knew the region, Julian took a force to Autun and repelled the invaders. Once on campaign, he decided to drive northward without delay, with a reinforcement of artillery and mailed cavalry. He paused briefly at Auxerre to refresh his troops and then continued on to Troyes—discovering and routing as he went marauding bands of barbarians, who were Germans known as Alamanni. From Troyes he pressed on to Reims, where he joined the forces assembled there under the command of Marcellus. From Reims Julian led the united army eastward to Metz and thence through the Vosges, while dispersing the barbarian groups he encountered and penetrating to the Alsatian plain they had occupied on the left of the Rhine. Julian learned that a series of Rhine settlements had fallen to the Alamanni, whose home territory lay on the other side of the river. The Alamanni now occupied sites from Strasbourg all the way to Mainz. In addition to those two places the intervening settlements of Brumat, Selz, Speyer and Worms were all in barbarian hands.

After a skirmish in a village of Lothringen Julian's force directly confronted the Alamanni on the occupied left bank of the Rhine. One fact, often forgotten but highly important for a clear comprehension of the Caesar's movements, is that simultaneously the emperor Constantius himself was marching through Switzerland from the south to cut off the Alamanni from the other side. It is evident that the two-pronged pincer strategy was not accidental but the result of concerted planning on the part of the emperor and his Caesar. The aim was the liberation of the Rhine from Alamannic control and on the whole that aim was achieved. Probably for this reason an attempt to repeat it was started the following year when Barbatio and his troops assumed, unsuccessfully, the role of Constantius' forces by moving into the region of Basel while Julian pressed toward Strasbourg by way of Zabern. In 356 Julian attacked the enemy at Brumat, north of Strasbourg, and after a success he then left the Alamanni to Constantius and turned with undiminished vigour to the north. Following the Mosel by Trier he advanced to Coblenz and Remagen, whence he achieved the recapture of Cologne. As we have seen, that event occurred ten months after the Franks had seized the colony, in other words no later than September of 356. It was a stunning climax to a season of strenuous and successful campaigning, of which an important part had been done in concert with the emperor.

Despite Julian's best efforts later to subvert the truth about 356 and despite whatever inner hostility he may have secretly felt, there can be no doubt that outwardly the emperor and his Caesar were working harmoniously together. Nor can there be any doubt that Julian commanded his own troops on his own authority. The bold plan to go directly to the lower Rhine after the recovery of Brumat was almost certainly his idea, a piece of ambitious daring that had nothing to do with the collaboration with Constantius' troops in Switzerland. The warlike enthusiasm which Julian instilled in his men was encouraged by a bounty which he placed on the heads of the German enemy. The taking of Cologne and the antecedent events along the Rhine reveal Julian in command. It was therefore inevitable that if Julian wished later to persuade the world of a subservient role malevolently assigned to him by Constantius up until 357, he would have to suggest that Cologne was not retaken before that year.

Constantius' faith in his Caesar appears to have continued unabated. After installing a garrison at Cologne, Julian returned south and made his winter quarters at Sens while Marcellus remained nearby with most of the troops. Julian was about to enter upon his second consulate, once again as a colleague of Constantius, when a barbarian force laid siege to Sens. It was only to be expected that Marcellus would have come to his aid with some part of the soldiery stationed outside the city, but no aid came. Marcellus, perhaps sulking in a spirit of jealousy over Julian's military successes in 356, refused to go to Sens. Nevertheless, with his own resources Julian managed after thirty days to bring an end to the siege. When Constantius received word of Marcellus' conduct, his response was quick and decisive. He discharged him from the army and ordered him back to his native Balkan town of Serdica (modern Sophia). Constantius' prompt dismissal of

Marcellus can only be explained by his support of Julian. Before returning to the Balkans Marcellus endeavoured to turn the emperor against Julian and to sow the seeds of discord, but—the fact is significant—he failed. Julian had providentially dispatched his trusted eunuch Eutherius to Constantius' court at Milan to speak in his defence and to rebut Marcellus' charges. Julian was accused of being headstrong and of attempting more than he was qualified to attempt.[9] These charges sound very much like the bitter resentment of an officer who has suddenly been eclipsed by a younger man.

Marcellus was replaced by the excellent Severus, and even Julian had to acknowledge that from this time he was now commander with his own authority. There could be no doubt on this score because Julian's most celebrated military triumph took place in 357, the so-called Battle of Strasbourg. Everyone knew this, in part because Julian himself wrote a monograph about it immediately afterward. He had not studied Caesar's Commentaries for nothing. It may well have been Julian's exploitation of his success near Strasbourg that first provided Constantius with a cause for anxiety and weakened the support he had so far unstintingly provided for his Caesar in Gaul.

With Barbatio, master of the infantry in succession to the worthy Ursicinus and himself an old enemy of Julian's disgraced half-brother Gallus, a pincer plan was devised along the same lines as in the previous year. Barbatio was to move from the south into the area of Basel while Julian and Severus marched eastward from Metz and Zabern to the Rhine in the vicinity of Strasbourg. Barbatio set out with a force of 25,000 men. In July Julian left Sens for Reims, and from there he headed for Alsace. The Alamanni, however, seized their opportunity, doubtless in the light of the wisdom they had acquired at such cost the year before. A horde of barbarians slipped easily through the exposed southwest sector between the armies to the south and west. They moved expeditiously as far as Lyons when Julian took swift action to cut off the routes of their return.

[9] Amm. Marc. 16.7.2.

If Barbatio was as jealous of Julian as Marcellus, it was nevertheless sheer incompetence that made his efforts so useless to Julian. Barbatio not only failed to prevent the return of the barbarian invaders through the territory which he controlled but he also failed to keep them from demolishing the bridge of ships which he was constructing to enable Julian's troops to cross the Rhine. Such folly, with so great a risk to Barbatio himself, can scarcely be considered wilful obstructiveness in a wicked scheme of Constantius to undermine Julian. Yet Julian later implied this, and many a modern reader has believed it. After his calamitous errors, Barbatio's forces were easily overwhelmed by the Germans, who then in triumph turned their attention to Julian.

The Caesar fixed upon Zabern as his camp and by giving his soldiers license to plunder the barbarian crops in Alsace built up a good store of provisions. The Alamanni sent envoys to Julian to protest: the land on the left bank of the Rhine was theirs to cultivate under the terms of their arrangement with Constantius. If he refused to respect the emperor's will, he was informed that war would follow. Undaunted and unprincipled, Julian had the envoys arrested as spies. It seems clear that he had resolved to remove the barbarian menace at the expense of repudiating Constantius' pledge, and in this decision we may legitimately see the first sign of Julian's independence of the emperor. The eager and arrogant nature of Julian underlies the provocation he gave the Germans by arresting their envoys. Militarily, however, his decision to drive them out of Alsace was unimpeachable. Constantius' arrangement with them had been made from weakness, and they had taken constant advantage of their foothold in Gaul.

The Alamanni massed their forces to a total of 30,000 or more. Julian waited for them with 13,000 men above the marshy ground on the left bank of the Rhine between Brumat and Bischweiler. With Severus and Julian in charge of cavalry on the left and the right flanks respectively, and with the infantry in the centre, the Roman army met the Alamanni. After a moment of trouble on Julian's flank, the Romans succeeded in driving back the enemy into the marshes and on into the river. Many swam in retreat or took refuge on islands. The Romans carried their pursuit on to those islands, and before the day was over they had captured Chnodomar, a king of the Alamanni. Later another king surrendered. In all some 6,000 Germans had fallen. Julian comported himself quite correctly in the aftermath of this great success, which we know by the name of the adjacent city as the Battle of Strasbourg. He sent Chnodomar to Constantius, who then celebrated a triumph on the occasion of Julian's victory. For centuries it had been customary for a reigning emperor to take the credit for a victory won in his name, and Constantius did nothing sinister in following this custom.

After the battle Julian went on to destroy the villages and ravage the land of the Alamanni who dwelt across the Rhine. It appears that he marched northward to punish those who had crossed over the Main to support their compatriots in the region of Strasbourg. He dispatched Severus to Cologne where a horde of Franks on the left bank of the river was causing havoc deep into Gaul. These barbarians were driven back into two forts on the river Maas, where Julian himself finally came to them in the winter of 357/8. After laying siege for fifty-four days, Julian starved them out and sent them to Constantius for service in the imperial army. With that accomplished he went to winter quarters in Paris, which became from that time his favourite place in Gaul.

In 358 Julian continued his resolute refurbishing of the Gallic frontiers. He addressed himself to the problem of the lowlands south of the river Maas. A nation of Franks (the Salii) had settled there in territory which had once been Roman. By encouraging an embassy from the barbarians to believe that they would be allowed to remain in that land, Julian lulled them into false confidence until he and Severus after rapid marches suddenly attacked them from the rear and compelled their submission without any major resistance. Julian then marched still further north into the land of the Chamavi, who dwelt between the Yssel and Rhine rivers. They sat astride the waterway along which corn was shipped from Britain to the Rhine, and they had been emboldened in recent years to impede the corn traffic. By rejecting the scheme of Florentius, the *praefectus praetorio* of the Gauls, to impose a high tribute on the Chamavi, Julian at once affirmed his preference for strong military action and incurred the lasting emnity of Florentius. The Chamavi were subdued, forts were placed on the lower Maas, and the fleet carrying corn from Britain was increased from 200 to 400 ships.

In the same year Severus crossed over the Rhine into the region of the Odenwald and overwhelmed still more German tribes. Julian himself appeared in person to receive the surrender of one native chief, Hortarius, and he imposed on the conquered people the task of rebuilding their destroyed cities and villages. By the end of 358 Julian had proved beyond all doubt that he was a cunning and efficient general. A master of diplomatic deception, a believer in conquest, swift, relentless, and ruthless, he turned northern Gaul back for a time into a sector of Roman domination, and by 358 that fact will not have escaped Constantius. The quarrel with Florentius over the taxation of the Chamavi was symptomatic, and it was to grow worse as Julian refused to cooperate with his praetorian prefect. The withdrawal of Severus at the end of the year may also indicate a new strain of arrogance and incompatibility in Julian, who, after all, owed much to that able colleague; but of this we cannot be sure for lack of evidence.

Julian's second and last panegyric of Constantius may be dated securely to the summer of 358 immediately after his lowland campaigns.[10] This represents, not without visible signs of strain, an attempt to proclaim his relations with the emperor as normal as before. If Julian was beginning by this time to envisage the possibility of open rebellion in view of his military strength and success, he must certainly have recognized that it would still be prudent to present himself as Constantius' man. Little did he realize that the Persians were already making demands that would soon lead to the emperor's complete preoccupation with troubles on the eastern frontier. The absence of Constantius in the East

[10] The proof lies at 56B, where Julian expressly states that he has had personal experience of the peoples who dwell along the sea coast. Thus the Batavian expedition of 358. The speech is no later than that year because at 66D the Persian king is said to be at peace.

would make things considerably easier for Julian in the West. For his part Constantius may have started to fear as much. It was not only that the insinuations of Julian's enemies at court may have seemed more credible. It was that Julian himself had let fall some unsettling remarks in the second panegyric. The piece opened with an allusion to the quarrel between Achilles and Agamemnon. Julian observed that Agamemnon failed to treat his general moderately and civilly. The Homeric citation is ultimately developed into praise of Constantius, but it looks very much as if Julian's deep concerns had been unconsciously divulged.

After another winter at Paris, Julian devoted much of the campaigning season of 359 to reconstruction and rehabilitation. He installed garrisons in important towns along the Rhine, including Neuss, Bonn, Andernach, and Bingen. At Mainz he dealt with a new incursion of barbarians and from there he made his way up the river. With the aid of Hortarius and some deception he won the submission of a number of additional German chieftains.

It was during these years of success in Gaul that Julian had the dream he described in confidence to his physician—the dream of the tall tree that bent over and collapsed while the fresh and flowering shoot alongside took firm root.[11] Clearly these were formative and influential years for the Caesar, who at the start had felt no shame in being the general of Constantius. Success and ambition altered his perspective and engendered exciting visions, prophetic and hortatory. Throughout all this period Julian had found time for the books in the library Eusebia had given him and for the few people he trusted and admired. The physician Oribasius was present with him, and so was an unnamed intimate whom he felt free to join in the secret practice of rites of paganism. With Maximus and Priscus he kept in touch by correspondence. And his panegyrics he submitted for approval to the teacher he had once been forbidden to hear, Libanius of Antioch.

In Gaul Julian found only one new friend, a counsellor (perhaps with the rank of quaestor) by the name of Saturninius Secundus

[11] See above, p. 17.

Salutius. This man, a Gallic native and presumably of considerable help to the Caesar in acquainting him with the Gauls and their country, was already of advanced age and apparently of Neo-Platonic sympathies. At any rate Julian looked up to him and depended upon him as a new Mardonius. This older mentor was snatched away by imperial order in the winter of 358/9, whereupon Julian composed an elaborate and intense discourse of regret on his departure.[12] Julian needed a man like this to lean upon, and Constantius may have anxiously recognized this trait in him. In 361, with Constantius buried, Julian brought Salutius back to be his praetorian prefect of the East precisely while he was there to launch his campaign against Persia. With Salutius and those few others—Oribasius, Maximus, and Priscus—he was hoping to repeat the military successes of Gaul. In vain.

[12] The name of Salutius appears as Sallustius in the manuscript tradition of this speech. Cf. Appendix III below.

CHAPTER FIVE

The Acclamation at Paris

In the winter of 359/60 marauding Scots and Picts disrupted the Roman peace in the north of Britain. Mindful of the fate of Constantius' brother, Constans, in a similar crisis, Julian rejected any idea of leaving Gaul himself in order to deal with the invaders, and he dispatched instead Lupicinus, the successor of Severus. Julian was consul for the third time in 360 and also for the third time had Constantius as a colleague. The relative quiet of Julian's operations in 359 together with the imposed departure of the influential Salutius may have encouraged the emperor, now embroiled in a struggle with the Persians and therefore far from the western part of his empire, to hope that he could rely on his Caesar in Gaul. If he did, in fact, entertain any such hope, he was soon to be undeceived.

Julian's successes had brought a substantial measure of peace and security to Gaul. His troops were now less active. Two auxilia, the Aeruli and Batavi, were turned over without danger to Lupicinus for his suppression of the Scots and Picts. Florentius had departed for Vienne to attend to the distribution of corn. An atmosphere of calm seemed momentarily to prevail, until—in February or March of 360—the tribune Decentius arived with a message from Constantius. Four auxiliary units, the Aeruli and Batavi as well as the Petulantes and Celtae (stationed in Paris), were instructed to depart forthwith for service in the East. In addition all other units were to provide 300 men each for the same purpose. This was a startling command. At a single stroke Julian was to be deprived of something like one-half or two-thirds of his army, and it was perhaps only natural that he should have thought some personal enemy, like Florentius, responsible for Constantius' decision to order the troops out of Gaul. Yet the military crisis on the eastern frontier was a perfectly reasonable explanation for the shift of troops from a front now calm to one that was not. To be sure, many of the soldiers ordered to leave were native Gauls. They were exceedingly reluctant to abandon their country and their families, and for Julian it became an embarrassment that he had once promised them they would never have to do so.[1]

The troops were assembled at Paris, and there they surged one evening round the residence of Julian, proclaiming him Augustus. The elevation of Julian by the soldiery to a rank hitherto enjoyed in recent years only by Constantius was inevitably a fateful step. The Caesar became co-emperor. Eutropius wrote some nine years later that this took place *consensu militum*, by the consent of the soldiers.[2] This suggests that the initiative did not come from them, whereas Julian and other writers tried hard to demonstrate that the soldiers forced his hand. The acclamation at Paris was a turning-point in Julian's career, and it is essential to ascertain, if possible, what really happened there. In any case one point is certain: Julian was spiritually ready for the promotion.

He disseminated his version of the acclamation in his message to the Athenians, composed in the autumn of the following year.[3] In it Constantius' order summoning the troops to the East appeared, probably accurately, as the main provocation. 'There was great excitement among the civilians and the troops', wrote Julian, adding that someone wrote an anonymous letter to some of the troops stationed near him with invectives against Constantius and with lamentations about his betrayal of the Gauls. The supporters of Constantius among Julian's advisers are said to have urged him to send all the troops off immediately before similar letters could be disseminated. Julian acceded, and on the

[1] Amm. Marc. 20.4.4.
[2] Eutropius 10.16. On what follows, cf. I. Mueller-Seidl, *Historische Zeit-schrift* 180 (1955), 225 ff.
[3] The relevant part is 283A–285A. Cf. recently I. Labriola, *Giuliano l'Apostata —Autobiografia* (1975).

advice of Decentius, who had brought Constantius' directive, all
the men to be dispatched to the East were assembled at Paris.
'The legions arrived', says Julian, 'and I, as was customary, went
to meet them and exhorted them to continue their march. For
one day they halted, and till that time I knew nothing whatever of
what they had determined; I call to witness Zeus, Helios, Ares,
Athene, and all the other gods that no such suspicion even entered
my mind until that very evening. It was already late, when about
sunset the news was brought to me, and suddenly the palace was
surrounded and they all began to shout aloud.' Julian relates that
in his uncertainty he prayed to Zeus, who obligingly gave him a
sign to accept the army's will. Julian would have the Athenians
believe that he was taken by surprise.

A few months later, at the beginning of January 362 in Constantinople, Mamertinus passed delicately over the details of
what had happened at Paris by suggesting that Julian's enemies in
the court of Constantius had stirred up enmity against him
through excessive praise of his accomplishments. Mamertinus had
travelled with Julian as he marched through the Balkans and preferred in his oration to evoke the stupefied faces of the peoples
there as they watched Julian go by like the Palladium dropped
down from heaven.[4] Libanius, however, welcoming Julian at
Antioch six months later, did not hesitate to pronounce a bene-
diction upon the soldiers' behaviour at Paris: 'Blessings upon
those soldiers who saw you crowned with victories and could not
forbear to place upon your head the jewelled crown! . . . Your
very valour invited its reward . . . This action, which they performed in consequence of what they regarded as necessity, was
ratified by the secret decisions of the gods . . . Ah, holy night,
inspired discontent of the soldiery and tumult more joyous than
any triumph!'[5] All the ingredients of the official version of the
story are here: Julian's innocence, the aid of the gods, the in-
evitability, and the desirability of what transpired. When, several
years later, Libanius composed his funeral speech for Julian he
undertook, in conformity with the vast scale of that speech, a

[4] Mamertinus, *Panegyr.* 6.4.   [5] Libanius, *orat.* 13.33–4.

more ample account of the Paris event; conceivably by then he also knew more about it. After the legions were gathered, Julian addressed them on the outskirts of the city, saying that Constantius' order could not be resisted. 'He spoke at length,' says Libanius, 'and they heard him in silence without saluting him at all, but during the evening, or rather about midnight, they gathered under arms, surrounded his headquarters and began to offer him the superior rank and title of Augustus.'[6] Libanius, who knew the letter to the Athenians as well as those now lost, failed to notice that according to Julian the soldiers surrounded his palace at sunset. Or perhaps Libanius was aware of discrepant stories, since his exact words are 'during the evening, or rather about midnight'.

Although Ammianus was not actually there in the spring of 360, he had access to first-hand information, and he was in a position to assess it on the basis of his own contacts with Julian before and after the events of that year.[7] He confirms Julian's report of an anonymous letter to the troops, and he quotes from it (or claims to). He confirms that it was on the advice of Constantius' man, Decentius, that the units were assembled at Paris. He confirms Libanius' report in the funeral speech that Julian addressed them on the outskirts of the city and urged them to obey Constantius' command. He seems to offer a compromise view on the timing of the soldiers' uprising, which he places in the earlier part of the night (*nocte . . . coeptante*). But Ammianus provides something new: between the allocution to the troops and the surrounding of the palace later there intervened the dinner hour, or more likely hours. As a gesture to the men about to depart for the East, we are told, Julian invited the officers of the soldiery to dine with him. They were hospitably received, and this only heightened their distress at leaving behind their commander-in-chief and their native Gaul.

The dinner with the officers recurs, not surprisingly, in Zosimus'

---

[6] Libanius, *orat.* 18.97. This speech can be dated to 365: cf. I. Hahn, *Klio* 38 (1960), 226 and A. F. Norman, *Libanius*, Loeb vol. 1 (1969), p. xxxiv.

[7] The incident occurs in Ammianus at 20.4.12–20.4.22.

account.[8] There we have some compromising details, which must be treated with respect inasmuch as they are presented by a historian whose bias is strictly pagan and favourable in general to Julian. After the dinner, Julian's military guests systematically prepared and distributed more anonymous letters to the troops, and these served to inflame a soldiery which—as Libanius told us —had stood in silence before Julian that very afternoon. Zosimus adds that in the evening the soldiers were quick to react to the letters because they had been relaxing with drink before their expected departure.

The coherent additions in the accounts of Ammianus and Zosimus provide items missing from the partisan reports issued in or soon after Julian's reign. They have an important implication—namely, of a conspiracy to incite the troops to declare Julian Augustus. It will be recalled that Photius judged Zosimus in this part of his history to be little more than an epitomator of Eunapius. It may therefore be assumed that the new material about the acclamation in Zosimus derives directly from Eunapius. This is equally true for Ammianus, now shown to have had access to the first edition of Eunapius' history. The supposition of a Eunapian origin for the officers' dinner and the leafletting is strikingly and firmly supported by the explicit testimony of Eunapius himself in the surviving *Lives of the Sophists:* Julian, he says, 'summoned a hierophant from Greece, and having with his aid performed certain rites known to them alone, he was emboldened to abolish the tyranny of Constantius. His accomplices were Oribasius of Pergamum and a certain Euhemerus of Libya... All of this has been described in fuller detail in my history of Julian.'[9] Here, then, is the Eunapian version in brief, and we know of course from Eunapius' own statement that the full account in his *History* was based on the memoir written for him by the scrupulous Oribasius himself. Thus, with the aid of

[8] Zosimus 3.9.
[9] Eunapius, *Lives of the Sophists* p. 476. The notion that Euhemerus was Julian's librarian is most implausible: it was proposed by G. W. Robinson, *Harvard Studies* 26 (1915), 165 ff. But the otherwise unknown Latin-speaking Carthaginian friend of Julian in Libanius, *orat.* 12.92 may possibly be Euhemerus.

Ammianus, Zosimus, and the surviving writings of Eunapius, we have succeeded in recovering an account of the Paris acclamation that comes from an intimate of Julian actually involved in what went on, a man who, with Julian dead, did not feel the pressure nor have by temperament the inclination to circulate a tendentious and incomplete story. He took pride in the achievement of the pagan intellectuals, among whom he had himself been outstanding in influence.

What happened, therefore, was this: the original anonymous letter addressed to the resident legions before all the others were gathered supplied the inspiration to Julian and his advisers. After Julian had been received in silence by all the legions on the outskirts of Paris, he, Oribasius, and a few others met at dinner with representatives of the troops and worked out the leafletting scheme, which was successfully put into effect that night. If one rereads Julian's letter to the Athenians with this knowledge in mind, one passage becomes more telling: Julian's advisers, disturbed by the original anonymous letter, urged him to dispatch the troops at once 'before similar letters could be scattered broadcast among the rest of the legions'. In other words, before what actually happened, happened. And when Julian protests that he knew nothing until that evening, he is probably telling the truth, simply not all of it. For during that evening the plan was hatched. It is doubtless because the dinner and the leafletting were omitted from the official, contemporary version of the incident that there arose some confusion over the exact time of night at which the soldiers surrounded the palace. Julian brought the time back to sunset to avoid too great a gap in the timetable of events. One ought not to dispute the genuineness of Julian's conviction that the gods were responsible for what occurred at Paris. Eunapius' version, with the calling of the Greek hierophant, underscores the fact. But the will of the gods was done through the agency of men, including the emperor himself: the soldiers were incited to riot. And so the challenge came to Constantius. As for Julian, now convinced of his destiny, we may recall a particularly apposite generalization of Gibbon: 'Whenever the

spirit of fanaticism, at once so credulous and so crafty, has in-
sinuated itself into a noble mind, it insensibly corrodes the vital
principles of virtue and veracity.'

Ammianus, characteristically blending the various items of the
sources he read, preferred to credit the testimony of his admired
Julian: *Caesar adsentire coactus est*, Caesar was compelled to agree.
In opting for tendentious fiction rather than the sordid details of
which history is so often made, Ammianus was shaping his work
of art with Julian as a prime exhibit. The drama at Paris had to be
presented with the conflict of the army's passionate appeal and the
Caesar's lofty restraint. Julian is assigned two speeches to the
troops in one of which he urges them to go to their homes,
promises they will never cross the Alps, and vows to intercede
satisfactorily with Constantius, whom he calls capable of reason
and highly sagacious. The same tone is maintained in the epistle
to Constantius, wherein Julian is made by Ammianus to inform
the emperor of the events at Paris. This long letter, which there is
no reason to regard as an authentic fragment of Julian's own
writings, shows a modest and respectful deputy of the emperor.
The flattery it contains is, however, reminiscent of Julian's panegyrics of Constantius, and it is by no means incredible that he
endeavoured to secure assent to his promotion by such a device.
Somewhat to the discomfort of readers of Ammianus, the letter
of Julian is interestingly complemented by an observation that
Julian sent in secret other letters to Constantius of a bitter and
accusatory kind.[10] These letters, says Ammianus, were not
available for scrutiny, and even if they were he thinks they ought
not to be made public. It is more than likely that they never
existed and that their existence had been maliciously alleged.
They are, in short, probably as fictional as the letter which
Ammianus does reproduce.

Constantius received word from Julian while at Caesarea in
Cappadocia.[11] It is reasonable to conjecture that he was installed
at the imperial palace there, which had ironically been Julian's

---

[10] Amm. Marc. 20.8.18: (*litteras*) *obiurgatorias et mordaces.*
[11] Amm. Marc. 20.9.1.

prison for six years of his youth. Upon hearing the news Constantius flew into a rage. He quickly recognized that he was no longer threatened only in the East by the Persians but now in the West by his own cousin. He resolved to face the Persians first but sent, in the meantime, his quaestor Leonas to Gaul with the clear message that Julian was still Caesar and should aspire to be no more than Caesar. Perhaps inferring that a cabal of officers must have given their support to the soldiers' action or at the least that the officers had not contained it, Constantius immediately sent out several replacements on Julian's staff. Among others, both Lupicinus and Florentius were withdrawn. They presumably should never have permitted such a thing to happen, and Lupicinus was judged to be proud and troublesome. Constantius underestimated, it seems, the influence of Oribasius, but that was because he never fully understood Julian's character. After all, Oribasius was just a blameless physician.

On 6 November 360, Julian was due to celebrate his quinquennalia, commemorating five years of imperial service. He was entitled to celebrate the occasion as Caesar, but in the West it looked more like the formal inauguration of his rule as Augustus. The coins are the best proof of this.[12] Both in anticipation of the quinquennalia and in celebration of the occasion the mints of Arles and Lyons produced coins proclaiming by legend and portrait two Augusti. On some pieces Constantius and Julian are named jointly with the title Augusti and with portraits of the two. On silver issues from Arles, Constantius and Julian are both represented while only the name of Julian is actually given—and that with the title Augustus. At Trier gold and silver coins were produced in the name of Julian Augustus alone. On issues from Arles and Lyons the *virtus exercitus* (or *exercitum* [*sic*]), the valour of the troops, was advertised. They had served Julian well on the whole, from the campaigns of 356 to that momentous night in the early spring of 360.

In writing his epistle to the Athenians in 361 Julian claimed that he had always decorously referred to himself as Caesar in his

---

[12] J. P. C. Kent, *Numismatic Chronicle* 19 (1959), 111.

correspondence with Constantius.[13] That may be, but in Gaul within months after the acclamation at Paris he was officially, if illegitimately Augustus. Publicly he treated Constantius as, at best, an equal.

[13] Julian 285D.

CHAPTER SIX

The Mask Removed

AFTER communications with Constantius which only exacerbated Julian's relations with him, the armies of Gaul, still full of enthusiasm and pride, were led by this new Augustus on a three months' campaign against some Frankish barbarians who had never before seen a Roman emperor. The action was designed to forestall criticism of Julian for lapsing into a haughty sloth and also to keep the soldiers in trim. Julian crossed the Rhine near Kleve in the flat country of the lower Rhine and subdued the Franks known as Attuarii. They had been ravaging the extremities of Gaul on the other side of the river. From the western lowlands Julian marched southeast to Basel. Although his route is not attested, passage through the Mosel valley by way of Trier is more than likely. It may well have been in connection with Julian's march to the upper Rhine that the Trier mint issued its gold and silver coins in the name of the new Augustus alone.

From the vicinity of Basel, where Julian expelled some Germans who had claimed possession of certain unidentified places, he went to Besançon. There, he asserted in the next year, he met a Cynic who reminded him in appearance of Maximus of Ephesus.[1] No doubt in retrospect he judged the similarity prophetic of his reunion with the eminent worker of wonders to whom he owed his conversion to paganism. From Besançon Julian passed further south to Vienne to spend the winter of 360/1 in the very city in which he had spent his first winter in Gaul. It was certainly an appropriate place for him to be on the occasion

[1] Julian, *Lettres* (Bidez), no. 26 [414D].

of his quinquennalia, 6 November. Leaving aside what appeared to be the prospect of unavoidable civil war with Constantius, Julian celebrated the anniversary with splendour. He did not forbear to wear a bejewelled diadem in addition to the imperial purple.[2] He was a very present Augustus.

The consuls who took office at the beginning of 361 were both Constantius' men. One, Taurus, was the praetorian prefect of Italy; and the other was Julian's old enemy, Florentius, now the praetorian prefect of Illyricum. Constantius must have hoped they would secure north Italy and the Balkans against Julian so as to isolate him in the west. The point was not lost on Julian, who by midsummer had devised a means of foiling his cousin's plan. Meanwhile, he attended to the affairs of Gaul and the strengthening of his support there. On Epiphany in January of 361 he took care to worship conspicuously in the Christian church of Vienne. The danger of openly observing paganism was still too great with Constantius alive, and by now Julian was skilled in concealing it. Furthermore, if we may judge from Ammianus, Julian was aiming at the broadest possible support for his usurpation and considered the profession of Christianity useful to that end. Later it was reported that the gods had reassured him of ultimate triumph by foretelling Constantius' death. A vision had come to him at midnight.[3] We may easily conceive that in this tense and dangerous season Julian was more receptive than ever to supernatural illumination.

While Julian was contemplating the forthcoming confrontation with Constantius, new trouble broke out in Gaul. It emerged that the barbarians had been solicited by Constantius to disturb the Gallic peace. According to Julian's account later in the year, the tribes had been bribed to devastate the land, and he managed to obtain copies of Constantius' incriminating letters.[4] He made clever use of the documents by reading out their contents whereever he went and winning over the appalled audiences to his own side. Constantius' behaviour in this crisis was an attempt to repeat his success against Magnentius, whose cause had been irreparably

<hr>

[2] Amm. Marc. 21.1.4.   [3] Amm. Marc. 21.2.2.   [4] Julian 286A–B.

damaged by the emperor's agreement to let the Germans move into parts of Gaul. The parallel of Julian with Magnentius must have seemed particularly striking at this time to knowledgeable observers, and probably even to Julian himself.[5] The coins and inscriptions of Magnentius had proclaimed him a liberator of the state, a bringer of freedom; and it is precisely the same characterization that dominates the inscriptions as well as the panegyrics of Julian. The *liberator rei publicae* is praised with equal enthusiasm by Mamertinus and Libanius.[6] What is more, Libanius, in a remarkable passage, speaks warmly of Magnentius' government when Constantius was at war with him.[7] In the west the parallel with Magnentius was obviously useful to Julian in 361, and provided important material for propaganda, but it was useful up to a point. Magnentius had been an unsuccessful usurper, whereas Julian wished to present himself, especially after Constantius' death, as the legitimate Augustus.

Vadomar, a king of the Alamanni, had been incited by Constantius to wreak havoc on the left bank of the Rhine alongside the southern part of the Black Forest. It was from this king, when apprehended, that Julian first learned of Constantius' treachery. The revelation naturally made him suspect some of the more recently appointed officers on his staff, especially Nebridius the praetorian prefect of the Gauls, whose refusal to swear allegiance to Julian roused the soldiery to attempt to murder him. Had it not been for the intercession of Julian himself, they would have succeeded. Under the circumstances a murder of the praetorian prefect would scarcely have aided his cause. On the other hand it had become obvious, to any who needed to know, what the soldiers felt about the partisans of Constantius. Nebridius fled. Julian imprisoned others.

A plan for staging the confrontation with Constantius was now

[5] Cf. W. E. Kaegi, *Byzantinische Forschungen* 2 (1967) [Festschrift Dölger], p. 248.

[6] For the coins of Magnentius: P. Bastien, *Le monnayage de Magnence* (1964). For the inscriptions, see the recent examples in *Epigraphica* 36 (1974), 187–8. On Julian as liberator: Mamertinus, *Panegyr.* 6.1; Libanius, *orat.* 13.41, 12.101. Cf. Appendix II below (the inscription at Ma'ayan Barukh).

[7] Libanius, *orat.* 18.33.

carefully worked out. Julian was fearful that if he marched eastward with his troops all together, the people of north Italy and the Balkans would judge his force too small to be taken seriously in a contest of such magnitude, He decided to move his men rapidly and in three separate operations so as to suggest a large and intimidating invasion. He entrusted one contingent to the cavalry commander Jovinus and to the quaestor Jovius, who were to pass into Illyricum by way of northern Italy. Another contingent, under the leadership of the cavalry commander, Nevitta, was to march by a middle route between the Alps and the Danube. Julian himself undertook to travel with 3,000 men through the southern Black Forest to the upper Danube and to move speedily in ships from the area of Ulm at which the river becomes navigable. In Gaul a certain Flavius Sallustius, trusted by Julian and in 363 raised by him to the consulate, remained as praetorian prefect to ensure the continued loyalty of the West to the new Augustus. Julian put no faith in the bishop Epictetus whom Constantius had sent him to guarantee his personal safety.

In July of 361 the triple march eastward began, and the scheme soon proved a resounding success. Constantius' key prefects, the two consuls Taurus and Florentius, fled together across the Julian Alps into central Europe. Meanwhile, with lightning speed —like a torch or fire-dart, wrote Ammianus[8]—Julian made his way down the Danube to the amazement of the natives. By early October he arrived at a town called Bononia, just north of the city of Sirmium (the modern Sremska Mitrovica), which had only recently been the residence of Constantius before his departure for Persia. The efforts of Lucillianus, Sirmium's commanding officer, to deter Julian from advancing were utterly unavailing, and Julian promptly entered the city to the enthusiastic greetings of the citizens. With lights, flowers, and prayers they hailed him as Augustus and led him to the royal palace of Constantius. Sirmium lay at a strategic point on the Danube, below the confluence with the Drave and just above the

---

[8] Amm. Marc. 21.9.6 (*ut fax vel incensus malleolus*).

confluence with the Save, in other words about sixty kilometres northwest of Belgrade. By his occupation of the place Julian acquired a secure grip on Illyricum.

The success of Julian's campaign thus far and the good will of the people of Sirmium were commemorated by festival games. At the same time Julian attended to the removal of Constantius' two legions which he had found there together with a cohort of archers. He dispatched them to Gaul, where he presumed they would be harmless; but unfortunately on their way to northern Italy they stopped at Aquileia, which was still firmly committed to Constantius, and they remained to swell the numbers of Julian's enemies in that city.[9]

Before leaving Sirmium, the new Augustus had occasion to meet Sextus Aurelius Victor, an author who only the year before had completed a compendious survey of the careers of all the Roman emperors down to Constantius. Victor had concluded his work with the expected eulogy of the reigning monarch, but his words had a curiously reticent quality. He managed to blend flattery of Constantius personally with a clear condemnation of Constantius' courtiers.[10] Since those courtiers were virtually united in their hostility to Julian, one may suppose that news of the acclamation at Paris had already reached Victor when he wrote the final lines of his work. Victor's gamble in attacking, however obliquely, the imperial court proved to be wise. When Julian met the historian in October of 361 he would not have been ignorant of his historical summary *De Caesaribus*. Shortly thereafter, he appointed Victor governor of Pannonia Secunda and honoured him with a bronze statue; in later years Victor rose to the prefecture of Rome.[11] Such was the clever and literate ally whom Julian opportunely acquired in the Balkans.

From Sirmium Julian and his forces moved southeast to Naïssus (the modern Niš), and there he remained from late October to early December. The delay was due to several uncertainties. The

[9] Cf. Kaegi, op. cit. (n. 5 above), p. 248.
[10] Aurelius Victor, *De Caesaribus* 42.25. Cf. Amm. Marc. 21.10.6 (on Victor and Julian).
[11] Cf. H. Dessau, *Inscriptiones Latinae Selectae* no. 2945.

resistance at Aquileia had to be overcome, and Jovinus was instructed to carry out that operation with the troops he had brought through northern Italy. Then Julian had to await the arrival of Nevitta's army as well as, in due course, that of Jovinus. There was in addition the business of explaining to the world why he was launching a civil war against Constantius. Now far from Gaul and the enclave of his partisans Julian had to win the allegiance of the rest of the Roman world.

This he undertook to do by writing elaborate and impassioned letters of justification to many of the major cities of Illyricum, Greece, and Macedonia, and to the senate at Rome. He had resolved to add the support of Italy and the Balkans to secure the territory which lay behind him as he moved on to meet Constantius. All of Julian's letters to the cities at this time have been lost with the exception of the one to Athens. But from that it is easy to judge the intense hostility toward Constantius which characterized these documents. The days of dissembling, of panegyrics, of calling himself only Caesar out of deference to the emperor were all over. No one could have mistaken the deep hatred which Julian at last displayed toward the man he accused of the murder of his family. The letter to the Athenians, like those now lost, was anything but a fair and impartial statement. It was firmly anchored in the tense and special situation of October and early November, 361. Julian's career and his life were at stake. The perilous enterprise begun at Paris was coming to a head.

Julian's success in gaining support was indicated not only by the gold coinage, issued in his name alone, from the mint at Sirmium, where he had been welcomed so cordially, but also by the gold minted at Thessalonica—again in his name alone.[12] Thessalonica was east and well to the south of Naïssus, and its enthusiasm may therefore be taken to prove the spreading of allegiance. On these coins from the time of Julian's residence at Naïssus the emperor appeared with a beard. Throughout his service in Gaul he had remained clean-shaven, for a beard gave the impression of a philosopher, and a pagan one at that. Julian's

[12] J. P. C. Kent, *Numismatic Chronicle* 19 (1959), 113.

beard in Illyricum, on which Mamertinus was soon to be so eloquent, was a first step in shedding the disguise he had been wearing in Gaul.[13]

Constantius had realized that he could no longer remain on the Persian front, and he was on his way back to confront the armies of his cousin when unexpectedly, at Mopsucrene in Cilicia, he died. At the age of forty-four Constantius gave no overt sign that he would die so providentially for Julian. Of course Julian had seen visions, and with Constantius' death their authority was suddenly made manifest. Death came to the emperor on 3 November, but the news did not reach Julian until the end of the month. The waiting and the anxiety abruptly ceased. Then at Naïssus in the city where Constantine, his detested uncle, had been born,[14] Julian found himself the sole emperor. He was jubilant, and he acted fast.

With the elimination of the Christian Augustus Julian felt that the gods had rewarded his long years of secret piety and devotion. Just as he had given up shaving and stripped away the pretence of respect toward Constantius, so now he stripped away the pretence of being a Christian. The deferential Christian Caesar vanished, and in his place stood the pagan Augustus. Julian publicly gave thank-offerings to the gods and held sacrifices. In a letter written at this time to Maximus of Ephesus, Julian reported, 'We worshipped the gods openly, and most of the army which accompanied me reveres them. We sacrificed oxen in public. We offered many hecatombs to the gods as expressions of thanks. The gods bid me to purify everything insofar as possible, and I obey them with enthusiasm. They say they will give rewards for our labours, if we do not grow slack.'[15] Many years later Ammianus claimed that Julian did not divulge the secret of his paganism until he

---

[13] Mamertinus, *Panegyr.* 6.4 (*inter illum pulveris qui barbam et capillum onerarat horrorem*). This decisive testimony was missed by F. D. Gilliard, who argued from coin portraits that Julian was smooth-shaven until his return to Constantinople: *Journal of Roman Studies* 54 (1964), 136. Coin portraits are not photographs and may well display features of an earlier date.

[14] See W. E. Kaegi's interesting article on Julian at Niš, *L'antiquité classique* 44 (1975), 161 ff.

[15] Julian, *Lettres* (Bidez), no. 26 [415c].

arrived at last in Constantinople,[16] but he is proved wrong out of Iulian's own mouth. The death of Constantius instantly removed the problems which had caused him to linger at Naïssus. Not that the future was without danger: times of transition are always dangerous, but Julian could now stop pretending and start to show the world what he was.

The first excitement over the news from Cilicia prompted Julian to write at once to many of the Greek intellectuals for whom he had special regard as well as to others upon whose support he thought he might be able to count. The long letter to his teacher and mentor Maximus was the most revealing, not only for its information about the public practice of paganism but also for the insight it provided into Julian's state of mind. He had had intimations of trouble which was threatening Maximus, presumably from the court of Constantius; and swearing by Zeus, Helios, Athene, and all the gods and goddesses he said that he had feared for him. He must have suspected that Constantius would move against the known associates of the rebel Augustus. 'I made inquiry of the gods, although I did not dare to do it myself—for I could endure neither the sight nor the hearing of what could possibly happen to you, so I made use of intermediaries.' Julian also went out of his way to tell Maximus that he had been proclaimed Augustus against his will 'as the gods know'.[17] They did of course, since Julian had prayed to Zeus to give him a sign on that fateful night. We should not doubt the sincerity of Julian's claim. He was neither the first nor the last ambitious man who, after making strenuous efforts to reach the goal he aspired to, humbly accepted the inevitable when he got there, murmuring 'Thy will be done'.

Julian also wrote to his mother's brother, who was another bearer of the name Julian. This uncle had been a Christian but had evidently by now been made privy to the secret religious life of the young Augustus, who must have suspected that his uncle had already turned pagan to support him (or would be willing to do

[16] Amm. Marc. 22.5.2.
[17] Julian, *Lettres* (Bidez), no. 26 [415A and 414B].

so). That is, in any case, what happened; and in later times Christian writers could point to the hideous death of the apostate uncle from intestinal worms as a just punishment of his apostasy. When Julian wrote to him from the Balkans, he said that thanks to the gods he was freed from experiencing or inflicting an irremediable blow. He called Helios and Zeus as witnesses that he never wanted to kill Constantius. 'Why then did I come? Because the gods expressly ordered me, promising salvation if I obeyed and that they would do nothing if I stayed. Above all as I was his declared enemy I thought only to frighten him and that matters would then turn to more agreeable negotiations. But if it had to be decided by battle entrusting everything to Fortune and the gods I determined to abide by their humane judgment.' Once again it is clear that in the euphoric aftermath of Constantius' death Julian's solicitation of support betrays the anxiety of his conscience.

To Eutherius, his faithful chamberlain, Julian recorded his salvation at the hands of the gods: 'Offer them sacrifices of thanks on my behalf. You will be sacrificing not for one man only but for the community of the Greeks (*hyper tou koinou tōn Hellēnōn*).'[18] Here we can see Julian's deliberate identification of his own cause with the cause of Hellenism everywhere. When he presented himself as the champion of the Greeks, there was already in his attitude no separation of Greek culture and pagan religion. As Gregory of Nazianzus was to object so vehemently, Julian identified Hellenism as a religion rather than a culture.

Among the other letters which Julian dispatched at this time were at least three to Christians, in which explicit thanks to the gods are conspicuously absent. Yet Julian must have realized early that he would have to come to terms in some way with Christian leaders, and these letters from the Balkans show that he chose the Christian recipients in the same way as the pagan ones. They were all persons with whom he had had previous connections, and therefore from whom he could have some hope of a favourable response. One was Aëtius, an unorthodox

<hr/>

[18] Julian, *Lettres* (Bidez), no. 29.

Christian but not of the conventional Arian persuasion, who had been an intimate of Gallus and as such known to his brother Julian. Aëtius had been exiled by the Arian government of Constantius, and Julian readily appreciated the support he stood to gain from dissident Christians. Another letter went to a certain Basil, who was in all probability Julian's former fellow-student from the days in Athens, Basil the Great, one of the Cappadocian fathers. Julian craved his presence, which would be much to his profit. The hypocrisy of a court was not to be the basis of Julian's association with his advisers, Basil was assured, but a free and open interchange. Basil clearly declined the invitation.[19] Another of the Christians whom Julian had seen at Athens received a letter,—Prohaeresius the eminent Armenian sophist. With a boldness verging on impudence Julian proposed to the great man that he write a sympathetic history of Julian's rise to power from documentary evidence to be supplied.[20] If Julian had succeeded in persuading his former teacher to undertake this work, his cause would have been wondrously advanced. No one could have resisted a history by a Christian sophist of the successful struggle of a pagan rebel against a Christian emperor.

In trying to assemble a group of counsellors, Julian encouraged not only the Christians, Aëtius and Basil, to come to him but, as was only to be expected, pagan sages. Naturally he pleaded with Maximus to come, as well as another Neo-Platonist, Eustathius. All those who were invited were offered the courtesy of the imperial transport system at Julian's express request. It is not known how many responded to the appeals sent out from the Balkans. Certainly Julian's circle of intimates was never in the months ahead to number more than the loyal and powerful trio of Oribasius, Maximus, and Priscus. The idealistic proposals with

[19] Julian, *Lettres* (Bidez), no. 32 [to Basil] and 46 [to Aëtius]. Bidez and others prefer to date these letters after Julian's arrival in Constantinople. The letter to Aëtius mentions Julian's amnesty for dissident Christians, but it is by no means clear that the new emperor waited until he reached the capital to announce the amnesty. The letters to Christians fit naturally into the context of his other letters from Niš after Constantius' death and commend the dating of the amnesty to that period. For further discussion, see below, p. 70.

[20] Julian, *Lettres* (Bidez), no. 31.

which he celebrated Constantius' death seem to have evaporated quickly. Besides, Julian himself arrived in Constantinople before most of his guests could have comfortably made their way to him either at Naïssus or on the march. Even Maximus waited to join him at Constantinople. Perhaps Julian's interest in seeing most of the people to whom he wrote did not last very long. Writing those letters was principally a means of putting his troubled conscience to rest.

Julian reached Constantinople on 11 December and there he received the satisfying report that the forces at Aquileia had finally declared for him.[21] The funeral of Constantius was held with great solemnity, as the new emperor made every effort to show his regard for the man he had not wanted to kill. He went into mourning while the body was still being transported from Cilicia, and when it arrived he helped to carry it with his own hands. In the procession he refused to wear the apparel of a monarch. Julian's concern to show proper reverence for his deceased predecessor sprang from several causes. Not least was the need to secure the troops who had served with Constantius in the East and felt loyalty toward him. There was also the question of legitimacy: Julian had to appear as the proper successor, not as a usurper, and he had therefore to display the tender regard appropriate to an heir. About this time a story began to circulate that on his deathbed Constantius had, in spite of everything, generously declared Julian his rightful successor.[22] Julian's conscience could rest more easily still.

[21] For the chronological problems of this time, see W. Ensslin, *Klio* 18 (1923), 116–18. I cannot accept all his conclusions, however.

[22] Amm. Marc. 21.15.5.

CHAPTER SEVEN

Justice and Reform

WITH Constantius in his grave and suitably honoured, Julian could turn to the problems of ordering the empire that now was his. There was much to correct and amend, and as always when power changes hands there was vengeance to be wrought. The favourites of Constantius and the enemies of Julian were endangered, although the new emperor showed himself willing, even eager to accept the allegiance of former partisans of Constantius who were prepared to do service under the pagan regime. It was to the punishment of the notorious spies and sycophants of his predecessor that Julian addressed himself in December of 361, once the resistance at Aquileia had yielded in response to the news that the old emperor was dead. Julian promptly set up a tribunal to judge a group of men who had formerly wielded great influence and had finally to face charges of abusing it. Julian himself was conspicuously absent from the panel of judges, perhaps to ensure fair and disinterested verdicts but more probably to free himself from direct personal responsibility for any decision that was unjust, yet politically desirable. The court sat at Chalcedon, on the Anatolian shore of the Bosporus opposite Constantinople.[1] Again the location may perhaps have been chosen to ensure that the judges would be unmoved by the pressures and gossip of the capital, but it is more probable that it was better suited to keeping the proceedings secret and uncontested.

The Chalcedon trials make perfectly good political sense for a new emperor in a still somewhat precarious position, but they cannot be invoked as proof of Julian's virtue and generosity of

---

[1] Amm. Marc. 22.3.2.

spirit. Libanius is at his least persuasive in suggesting that the purges of December 361 were so few as to make one marvel at Julian's restraint.[2] The sophist of Antioch was not wrong in implying that the responsibility for what went on at Chalcedon was really Julian's but he deluded himself in praising the emperor for what he did. The composition of the tribunal and the judgments handed down were no cause for panegyric. In addition to revealing Julian's efforts to wipe out troublesome opponents and to settle some old scores they betray—under the guise of justice—his weakness in respect to the army.[3] The Chalcedon tribunal was a military tribunal, and its decisions represented first and foremost the decisions of the army. Without the confidence and support of the troops, his own and those of Constantius, Julian's reign would have been over before it began.

The judges at Chalcedon were all soldiers themselves, and their deliberations were conducted in the presence of the officers of the armies of the Joviani and Herculiani.[4] To serve as the presiding magistrate Julian appointed his trusted friend from the years in Gaul, Salutius Secundus, now promoted to the important office of praetorian prefect of the Orient. Highly intelligent and sympathetic to Julian, Salutius could be trusted to give opinions which were in Julian's interest. When these, however, clashed with the opinions of the army, the latter would prevail; and Salutius had to agree, because the support of the army was also in Julian's interest. Of the five other judges, four were experienced officers, Nevitta, Jovinus, Agilo, and Arbitio. The first two of these were proven supporters of Julian and had only recently led divisions of his army from the West, but for all that they were soldiers (Ammianus thought Nevitta crude, uncultivated, and cruel);[5] and they found no difficulty in sharing views with Agilo and Arbitio, both of whom had been supporters of Constantius. Some have seen in

---

[2] Libanius, *orat.* 18.153.
[3] Cf. W. E. Kaegi, *Byzantinische Forschungen* 2 (1967) [Festschrift Dölger], 251 ff.
[4] Amm. Marc. 22.3.2.
[5] Amm. Marc. 21.10.8 (*inconsummatum et subagrestem et [quod minus erat ferendum] celsa in potestate crudelem*).

Julian's selection of these two men evidence of his impartiality; yet his need to secure the adherence of the armies of Constantius had made it imperative to choose representatives of those forces. Agilo, it appears, was a person who had accepted with equanimity the fact of Julian's elevation. Born among the Alamanni, he must have had good reason to respect Julian's military prowess. Less respectable was Arbitio, an old intriguer who had been close to Constantius' provincial chamberlain, the eunuch Eusebius. Julian's appointment of the worthless Arbitio to the panel at Chalcedon can only have been a concession to the troops of Constantius. Since Arbitio had marched against Julian in the civil war, he might have more readily been a defendant than a judge.

Mamertinus, consul designate for 362 and the author of the extant Latin panegyric of Julian, was the only other member of the Chalcedon tribunal. He had risen rapidly in Julian's service to become praetorian prefect of Illyricum and Italy, and it was he who tried the rebels at Aquileia just before commencing his labours at Chalcedon. Clearly he was another upon whom Julian hoped to rely. Mamertinus' role was no less tricky than it was for Salutius, Nevitta, and Jovinus; the delicacy and awkwardness of his assignment is likely to be the reason he said nothing about it in his panegyric, a work which is not distinguished by modesty on the part of the speaker. There can be no doubt that the trials were already underway when Mamertinus became consul on January the first and delivered his speech, since Ammianus has recorded the humiliation of Taurus, consul of 361, who was called to stand trial still in the year of which he was an eponym.[6]

Among the defendants at Chalcedon were two of the most hated spies of Constantius, Apodemius and Paul (known by the ominous nickname of 'the chain'). There was no one to bewail the incineration of these once feared agents. Nor did justice seem to be wanting in the condemnation and elimination of the eunuch Eusebius. The judgments delivered against two of Julian's old antagonists in Gaul, Florentius and Taurus (who happened both to be consuls in 361), seemed more obviously designed to put the

[6] Amm. Marc. 22.3.4.

new emperor at peace. Even Ammianus cannot suppress an objection to the condemnation of a man who simply remained loyal to his emperor. Alleged enemies of Julian's brother Gallus were also summoned before the tribunal—presumably to exact vengeance for old affronts which Julian considered part of Constantius' hostility to his family. It had already been evident in the letter to the Athenians that while Julian was willing to acknowledge cruelty and excess in the behaviour of Gallus he nevertheless considered the removal of his brother a vindictive act of Constantius and his court. The Chalcedon jury condemned one man for contributing to Gallus' fall and acquitted another.[7]

For Ammianus and for subsequent historians it was the condemnation of Ursulus which constituted an undeniable miscarriage of justice. This man had been in charge of the treasury in Gaul when Julian was there, and he had signally assisted the young Caesar by ordering that whatever funds he required be provided at a time when some of Constantius' officers were attempting to hinder Julian's progress. Both Ammianus and Libanius make it plain that Ursulus was a victim of the army, which had hated him ever since he had been heard to utter some indiscreet remarks at the siege of Amida several years earlier.[8] The condemnation of a man who had helped Julian at an important moment in his career brought him the charge of ingratitude and demonstrated beyond any doubt that he had to oblige the military to survive. It is instructive to remember that of the six judges at Chalcedon, only two had been supporters of Constantius in the civil war. Evidently some or all of Julian's own partisans pronounced the destruction of Ursulus. Justice herself, as Ammianus phrased it, seemed to weep.[9] By virtue of his absence from Chalcedon, Julian was able to take a different position from that of the judges and to acknowledge the wrong they had done by making restitution to Ursulus' daughter of her father's property. But Ursulus was none the less dead, and the officers well pleased.

[7] On the verdicts, Amm. Marc. 22.3.
[8] Amm. Marc. 22.3.8; Libanius, *orat.* 18.152. At Amida Ursulus was heard to comment on the greed of the soldiery (Amm. Marc. 20.11.5).
[9] Amm. Marc. 22.3.7 (*ipsa mihi videtur flesse Iustitia*).

The Chalcedon trials afford the most direct glimpse into the unsteady position of Julian immediately after Constantius' death, and they prove that Julian's policies could be based upon political considerations just as much as principles. One can easily see in the new sole monarch the same combination of pragmatist and visionary that was the architect of the Gallic campaigns. While the tribunal at Chalcedon was determining the fate of Paul the Chain, Ursulus, and others, the provinces of the empire were receiving word of two of Julian's most celebrated measures. These were the first stages in the overthrow of the Christian state and the fulfilment of Julian's most cherished dream, the recall of the pagan gods to their ancient splendour. Julian proclaimed the reopening of the pagan temples and the restoration of pagan worship through sacrifices.[10] He also proclaimed universal religious toleration, including an amnesty for orthodox Christians who had been driven into exile by the Arian government of Constantius.[11]

These drastic measures appear natural enough in the context of Julian's spiritual development, but at the time only a small number of intimates were privy to that development. So consistently and so successfully had Julian concealed his change of faith. The actual dates of the edicts of restitution and amnesty are not recorded, but their dissemination in the empire implies that they were issued just as soon as Julian felt in a strong enough position to make his personal paganism public. Since he began to sacrifice publicly while he was still in the Balkans on his way to Constantinople, it is more than likely that the edicts were issued from Naïssus along with the invitations to eminent intellectuals of the East. They would belong to the euphoria and sense of triumph which came with the news of Constantius' death. At the latest, the edicts can be dated to Julian's first days in Constantinople, as Ammianus' narrative suggests. Ammianus, however, was under the mistaken impression that Julian did not divulge his own paganism until that time.[12] It makes better historical and psychological sense to

---

[10] Amm. Marc. 22.5.2. Cf. Libanius, *orat.* 18.126.
[11] Julian, *Lettres* (Bidez), no. 46 [404B]. Cf. Sozomen 5.5.9.
[12] Amm. Marc. 22.5.1–2.

place Julian's momentous pronouncements precisely in Naïssus.

Julian envisaged a pagan empire, not merely in which pagans were free to practise their religion but in which paganism was the state religion. This inescapable fact means that the general amnesty must not be considered simply as a generous and benevolent gesture but rather as a deliberate effort to neutralize the Arian establishment of Constantius by restoring its old and formidable enemies, such as the bishop Athanasius. We need not accept Ammianus' extreme cynicism in attributing Julian's measure to an expectation that the Christians, being naturally more contentious than wild beasts, would destroy one another.[13] It was quite sufficient in late 361 to eliminate the monopoly of the Arians and perhaps even for a short while to win the good will of the restored orthodox, to several of whom Julian made friendly overtures. But the orthodox were to look in vain for any further help from Julian. As he carefully explained in the case of Athanasius, he had granted a return from exile but not a restoration to episcopal sees.[14] The amnesty was proclaimed so that the power of Constantius' Christians might be weakened. Thus paganism could flourish again.

When Julian turned his attention, upon his arrival in Constantinople, to the complex organization of the court as he inherited it from Constantius, the reforms he instituted are also best explained in terms of his own personality and predilections. But Gregory of Nazianzus was wrong to assume that the ultimate objective of the court reforms was the elimination of Christians who had served Constantius.[15] Gregory did not take adequate account of Julian's intolerance of luxury, bureaucracy, and ceremonial. Constantius had nourished a teeming hive of slaves and eunuchs, petty functionaries and flatterers, whose trifling tasks were grotesquely disproportionate to their personal magnificence. Although some saw in this ostentation an appropriate reflection of the imperial majesty, a man of Julian's austere and ascetic temperament found

---

[13] Amm. Marc. 22.5.4.
[14] Julian, *Lettres* (Bidez), no. 110 [398D].
[15] Greg. Naz., *orat.* 4.64 [Migne, *PG* 35. 106B].

it naturally abhoirent. The Christian courtiers of Constantius were not removed to make way for pagans. They were simply cleared out like so many unsightly weeds. Libanius' account of what Julian found in the court is exaggerated but, as an impressionistic evocation, basically truthful: 'There were a thousand cooks, as many barbers, and even more butlers. There were swarms of waiters, more eunuchs than flies around cattle in springtime and a multitude of drones of every sort and kind.'[16] When Julian summoned a barber one day, a man appeared so sumptuously attired that he looked more like a high officer of the treasury.[17] All this was deeply offensive to a monarch who preferred to sleep on straw, hated theatres and games, and had no use for sex. He therefore swept away the infestation of the court.

Along with cooks, barbers, and butlers Julian also cleared out other rank growths of a more poisonous kind; and he cannot have been unaware that by removing hordes of imperial spies, known as *agentes in rebus*, as well as highly influential secretaries (*notarii*) he was not only ending many widespread abuses in the empire but also making the channels of communication between himself and his appointees far more open. The self-serving villainy of the spies and secretaries is documented at such length by Libanius as to suggest considerable experience of them. Their intrigues and blackmail had blighted the Christian empire, and Julian fully deserved the gratitude of the provincials for suppressing them.

While purging the retinue of Constantius Julian undertook to restore the senate of Constantinople, which he found oppressed and impotent, to its proper dignity. It can scarcely be doubted that Julian had hopes for securing a base of power in the senate, of which he insisted he was himself a member, but his concern also reflects a genuine conviction that cities should be able to look after their affairs through the enlightened and honorable service of local councillors. The senate at Constantinople was not much different from the councils of many other Greek cities in the diminished prestige of its members. It was more fashionable and

---

[16] Libanius, *orat.* 18.130. Cf. Amm. Marc. 22.4.
[17] Amm. Marc. 22.4.9.

certainly more lucrative to avoid service, with its financial burdens, than to undertake it. Julian, with his good knowledge of earlier imperial history and the importance of the city councils (not to mention the Roman senate) in previous centuries, strove in this respect, as more notoriously in others, to turn the clock back. He did not foresee the opposition of those special-interest groups prospering under the system he wanted to change, nor his own death in just over a year. His edicts survive only as pointers to an overall reform he never achieved.

He explicitly enunciated the right of every senator to be considered innocent and free until such time as he was actually convicted of wrongdoing. Julian's edict of February, 362, opens with these striking words: *Ius senatorum et auctoritatem eius ordinis, in quo nos quoque ipsos esse numeramus, necesse est ab omni iniuria defendere* ('The right of the senators and the authority of that class in which I also count myself must be defended from every injustice.')[18] An edict of the following month took away certain menial tax-collecting responsibilities from senators as unworthy of their dignity.[19] Julian took pains to go himself to meetings of the senate rather than, on occasion, to summon senators to the palace, as Constantius used to do.

To strengthen the councils of the Greek cities in the provinces Julian enlarged the allowed number of members in certain cases so as to permit service by all who were qualified.[20] He then reduced the possibilities for exemption and opened up membership to many formerly disqualified—as, for example, by possessing an appropriate family background on the mother's side only or by being citizens of one city and residing in another. It is within the context of these efforts to build up the Greek cities into the *poleis* of earlier ages, with authoritative and prestigious councils, that Julian's revocation of the exemptions for Christian clergy should be seen. On 13 March 362, Julian proclaimed that no one could henceforth claim exemption from service as a *decurion* (councillor)

[18] Cod. Theod. IX. 2.1.
[19] Cod. Theod. XI. 23.2.
[20] Julian, *Misop.* 367D; cf. Libanius, *orat.* 18.148 and *epist.* 696.

on the grounds of being a Christian.[21] Since only the clergy had been entitled to seek an exemption, the measure was accordingly directed at them. It was less an anti-Christian move than an attempt to restore affluent and intelligent citizens to the local councils, which had need of both their intelligence and their money. It was, however, a clever way to divert ecclesiastical profits to the cause of the revival of Greek cities.

There are indications from the edicts of Julian as preserved in the Theodosian Code that in those first months of sole rule he was endeavouring on many fronts, minor as well as major, to simplify the bureaucracy of the empire and thereby to facilitate a return to traditional Hellenism. The correction of notable abuses in the financial organization of the provinces was presumably not only an effort to win applause but a means of stimulating the economy by returning more funds to the cities. Julian's indifference to wealth and luxury made him incorruptible in the matter of money, and for his short reign he tried valiantly to see that available resources were put where they were most needed.

Much praised was his restitution of city properties which had been seized improperly and occupied. Although Christian writers saw in this measure a device to strip the Church of some of its land, it is evident that Julian's chief purpose was to provide the cities with additional sources of revenue from leasing of the restored territories. This aim is explicitly stated in his edict of 15 March 362, in which he orders the restoration of *possessiones publicae* to the cities so that they can be leased at fair rates *quo cunctarum possit civitatium reparatio procurari* ('to make possible the recovery of all the cities').[22] Again in the interest of strengthening the cities Julian eliminated the burdensome expense of the *aurum coronarium*. It had become traditional for the cities of the empire to vie with one another in providing golden wreaths annually to the emperor, and the competition to give the heaviest weight had led to an excessive expense which Julian reasonably thought the cities could do without. The *aurum coronarium* was made strictly voluntary by an edict of 29 April 362.[23] It is possible

[21] Cod. Theod. XII. 1.50.   [22] Cod. Theod. X. 3. 1.   [23] Cod. Theod. XII. 13.1.

that Julian refused to take the obviously more effective step of banning such gifts altogether in view of their traditional character and their significance in the relations, so often jealous, between cities. Certainly some cities continued to give golden wreaths, and Julian indulged them.

Another of the local financial burdens which Julian hoped to alleviate was the cost of maintaining the imperial courier system (*cursus publicus*) which provided animals and equipment for authorized persons travelling throughout the empire. Abuse of the *cursus publicus* was nothing new, and emperors since Tiberius had done their best to prevent it.[24] In the fourth century the *agentes in rebus* were notoriously hard on the animals, which, according to Libanius,[25] often dropped dead at the end of a journey. It was the cities which bore the cost of provisioning the system. Apart from cutting out the spies who had been the most abusive patrons of the *cursus publicus*, Julian introduced very stringent regulations as to journeys for which the official animals could be used. He controlled the number of permits (*evectiones*) and restricted those who could issue them to a few high-ranking officials in addition to himself.[26] Julian's own use of the *cursus publicus* after Constantius' death can be observed in some of his letters of invitation to the distinguished intellectuals he wished to have with him. To Aëtius and Eustathius he offered the convenience of government transportation.[27] Julian's reform of the *cursus publicus* appears to have been at least momentarily successful. Libanius paints a bright picture of healthy horses and mules.

The tax collectors of the imperial treasury were given formal notice that after every five years of work they were to have one year free so as to be open to prosecution from any who cared to bring complaints against them.[28] Those guilty of fraud were to be

[24] See S. Mitchell, *Journal of Roman Studies* 66 (1976), 111–12.
[25] Libanius, *orat.* 18.143.
[26] Cod. Theod. XIII. 5.12. Cf. Libanius, *orat.* 18.145. For further documentation, see W. Ensslin, *Klio* 18 (1923), 135 ff.
[27] Julian, *Lettres* (Bidez), no. 34 and no. 35 (Eustathius), no. 46 (Aëtius).
[28] Cod. Theod. VIII. 1.6.7.

subject to torture—as much an indignity as a discomfort. In certain individual cases Julian reduced the tax assessment of cities or cut back the amount of arrears still owing. In March of 362 he announced that no imposition of new taxes nor remission of old was to be laid upon any of the provincials without being first referred to him personally for review.[29] Such direct involvement of the emperor in financial affairs was an inevitable and undoubtedly intended result of the reduction of the bureaucracy of Constantius.

An extant letter of Julian to the Thracians illustrates clearly the operation of his March edict on taxes.[30] In response to a request for a cancellation of debts owed to the treasury the emperor declared that it was not his aim to amass funds from his subjects but to help them as much as possible. Accordingly he annulled the indebtedness of the Thracians but required them to turn over half the sum formerly owed for the benefit of the soldiers in the region—which, he said, would ensure peace and safety. This clever decision, obliging the provincials and securing payments to troops at the same time, was ultimately of course to the advantage of the troops since the Thracians still had to pay, if only half of what they had hoped to be forgiven.

The adroitness and sophistry of Julian's remarks to the Thracians were generally characteristic of his administration in the first months of sole rule. The Chalcedon tribunal, the restitution and amnesty edicts had set the tone of cunning candour, self-righteousness, and ostentatious fairness. But, just as at Chalcedon or in his letter to the Thracians, matters were not always so straightforward as they sometimes appeared to be. Julian was an experienced dissembler, always in what he judged to be a good cause. His treatment of a group of Egyptian petitioners, as recorded by Ammianus, provides a particularly clear view of Julian the statesman soon after Constantius' death.[31] The Egyptians, almost certainly Alexandrians in view of the contentious disposition which Ammianus assigns to them, took advantage of

---

[29] Cod. Theod. XI. 16.10.   [30] Julian, *Lettres* (Bidez), no. 73 [428C–D].
[31] Amm. Marc. 22.6.

the change of emperors to claim repayment of moneys they had
been compelled to pay, justly or unjustly, for the past seventy
years. The petitioners pressed their absurd demand not only upon
the praetorian prefect but also upon the young emperor himself.
Julian's response, if not honest, was at least as levantine as the
behaviour of the Egyptians. He instructed them to go over to
Chalcedon whither he promised he would come to adjudicate their
complaints. Once all the Egyptians had had themselves ferried
across to Chalcedon, Julian issued firm orders to the boatmen
who transported passengers across the Bosporus that no Egyptian
was to be taken on board. Thus the band of petitioners was
isolated from the emperor and left to calm down. After waiting in
vain at Chalcedon they finally all went home.

No one would question the unreasonableness of the Egyptians'
demands nor the efficiency of Julian's bizarre way of handling
them. He will have considered his conduct necessarily devious,
but those who observed it could not have been reassured. Julian
was always sure he knew what was right and acted, even dis-
honestly, in accordance with it. Justice and reform which were
based upon the moral perceptions of one man were nothing less
than an attempt to shape the world in his image. Julian's character
and ideals were not to everyone's taste, not indeed to most
people's taste. Whatever integrity and whatever justice informed
the administrative measures of the early months of his reign as
sole emperor—and much of his achievement then was admirable
—originated in personal attitudes, passionately maintained. His
own religiosity, asceticism, and political acumen underlay his
actions and his edicts. An administrator with so strong a personality was bound to run into trouble and to deteriorate as soon as the
opposition could unsettle him. A weaker man would have survived.

It is striking that when Ammianus catalogued the virtues of
Julian at the conclusion of his narrative of the reign, he recorded
under the rubric of *liberalitas* the reduction of tribute, the policy
on the *aurum coronarium*, remission of debts, improvement in pro-
cedures for handling complaints involving the imperial treasury,

restitution of property and the income from it to the cities.[32] These are all measures which, in their original form, antedate Julian's final year as emperor. Ammianus notes that on the topic of imperial finances Julian liked to quote one of his great models, Alexander the Great, who, when asked where he kept his treasury, replied, 'With my friends.' But Alexander's fortunes altered rapidly, and he died at thirty-two.

[32] Amm. Marc. 25.4.15.

CHAPTER EIGHT

The Puritanical Pagan

AMMIANUS was unaware that Julian and his troops openly worshipped the pagan gods once the news of Constantius' death had reached them in the Balkans. At the end of 361, when Julian was in Constantinople, the revival of paganism did not begin, as Ammianus claimed; rather it gathered strength, and the aims of the new emperor were unmistakable. His edicts of restitution and toleration suggested that perhaps a new era of genial polytheism was dawning, but anyone who had knowledge of Julian's personality would not have taken such a prospect seriously. Even Mamertinus in his New Year's address of January 362 had to meet objections that this dedicated pagan might wish somehow to impose on his subjects the strictly disciplined piety of his own life. The soldiers from Gaul were already joining him in sacrifices, and the court of Constantius had been quickly purged of its Christian voluptuaries. Reports of the unreliability of the eastern armies of Constantius must have been grounded, at least in part, in the expectation that they would have to turn pagan or suffer the consequences. In the first months of his reign Julian courted the Christians with assurances of toleration and an ostentatious regard for the deceased emperor. But a man with a strong faith in what he believed to be the only true religion was not likely to do much to advance the cause of those he considered ungodly. For Julian the ungodly were the Christians.

The asceticism and inflexibility of Julian's style of life were integral to his practice of paganism. Under Constantius luxury had grown up in the Arian court and spread among the clergy and citizens of the Christian world. Bishops grew fat from the

revenues of ecclesiastical property and spent in cultivated reading
the leisure to which they were entitled by civic immunities. At
Syrian Antioch a largely Christian city passed its time in the
excitement of the theatre and chariot-racing. There was nothing
romantic or colourful about the paganism which Julian proposed
to establish in the place of the religion of Constantine. Its austerity
and the fanatical zeal of its advocate portended the end of the way
of life which had not only replaced the old paganism but actually
absorbed its *joie de vivre*. The deadly earnestness of Julian was
manifest and unwelcome. Those who stood to gain, men like
Maximus and Oribasius, as well as those opportunists who saw
political success in a timely renunciation of Christianity, were not
numerous. Julian's court was never crowded with counsellors,
and his reign bore from the start the clear imprint of his character.

When Alexandria in Egypt became the scene of rioting in late
December of 361, the Arian bishop, George of Cappadocia, whose
library had once afforded Julian so much edification during the
years of exile, was murdered. The new emperor responded to this
act of violence in a manner which ominously adumbrated his
response to violence against Christians later in the reign. He inflicted no punishment. Ammianus obscures the significance of this
incident in several ways—by dating it a year after it occurred (and
thus to a more turbulent season in Julian's short reign), by implying that hostilities between Arian and orthodox Christians were at
issue, and by indicating that intimates of the emperor dissuaded
him from taking proper action in view of the internal struggles of
the Christian community.[1] But it is clear from Julian's letter to
the Alexandrians in regard to the murder of George that his
refusal to punish was due principally to satisfaction over the
elimination of an 'enemy of the gods'.[2] Julian rebuked the people
of Alexandria for taking justice into their own hands when they
could simply have had George condemned in court for his misdeeds (as the Alexandrians judged his actions to be). George
deserved to be put to death, according to Julian; but pious devotees
of the gods ought not to go to worship with blood on their hands.

[1] Amm. Marc. 22.11.3–11.   [2] Julian, *Lettres* (Bidez), no. 60 [379c].

That was the fault of his murderers, whom, incidentally, he clearly believed to have been pagan. But it was good to have George out of the way; and, forswearing punishment, Julian merely reminded the Alexandrians that they were Greeks of ancient stock. He anticipated that henceforth they would conduct themselves worthily of that Greek character he so much admired.

Julian's handling of the Alexandrian riots of late 361 showed to anyone of sense that the new emperor was not about to protect the rights of Christians. Worse still, he believed that they merited extirpation, though not by illegal means. Within a few months Julian made his views even clearer in a group of philosophical essays which could perhaps be better described as encyclicals. These works, composed by the emperor himself at Constantinople in the spring of 362, make it impossible to imagine that he ever envisaged a world in which religious toleration and concord were the policy of the state. The notion, sometimes widely accepted, that Julian's objectives in the early months of his reign were different from those later is wholly indefensible.

The essays of spring 362 appear to have been provoked in the first instance by opposition to Julian from pagan philosophers of the Cynic school. These outspoken and ill-kempt gadflies of society, whom Constantius had endured with equanimity, roused Julian to a fury.[3] Not only did they attempt to criticize his administration and thereby to expose dissent among the pagan ranks, but they also laid claim to superior philosophical wisdom. As a Neo-Platonist Julian resented this intellectual assault and undertook to inform the Cynics of his day that they were nothing but fraudulent apes of Cynic manners and dress. He charged them with affecting simplicity and poverty while being guilty of greed and sensual indulgence. The emperor insisted on the unity of truth and philosophy: 'Let no one divide philosophy into many kinds or cut it up into many parts . . . For even as truth is one, so too philosophy is one.'[4] In other words, there were not to be rival schools of philosophy, but only the right philosophy; and Julian made plain that he knew which the right one was. The true Cynic

[3] Cf. Julian 223D.   [4] Julian 184C.

was a person of whom he could approve, indeed a person remarkably like himself: 'He who enters upon the career of a Cynic ought first to censure severely and cross-examine himself, and without any self-flattery ask himself the following questions in precise terms—whether he enjoys expensive food, whether he cannot do without a soft bed, whether he is the slave of rewards and the opinion of men.'[5] Julian's hostility to other forms of paganism than his own showed the character of a bigot and a puritanical one at that. His ample discourse addressed to the 'Uneducated Cynics' was written at white heat—in two days, by his own admission.[6]

Two related works of the same period were composed in one day each. They are immensely revealing. One was a reply to a particular Cynic by the name of Heracleius, and the other a meditation on the mother of the gods, Cybele. In the piece to Heracleius Julian again denounced the Cynics of his day as fraudulent copies of true Cynics, men who seek honour, wealth and preferment through the affectation of poverty. The emperor had long had a name for these ostentatious beggars—'monks', a name, he observes with savagery, used by the impious Galilaeans for those who suffer small inconveniences in the hope of large gain.[7] This allusion to the Christians is uncompromisingly hostile. They are *dussebeis*, impious. Later, in the same discourse, Julian developed an elaborate myth to describe his own career under the care of *Helios*, the sun. Zeus instructs Helios to care for the young child, who is Julian, and to cure him of his disease (*nosos*), which is clearly his Christian faith. Subsequently Helios tells the child that his destiny is to cleanse away all impiety (*asebēmata*).[8] There can be no doubt that as early as spring of 362, and almost certainly well before that, Julian looked forward to the ultimate eradication of Christianity.

Julian's essay on the mother of the gods is an illustration of his own piety. A reverent treatment of the emasculation and salvation of Attis led the emperor to consideration of the dietary needs of the faithful. Once again the asceticism which Julian prescribed for

---

[5] Julian 200B–C.   [6] Julian 203B.   [7] Julian 224B (*apotaktistai*).
[8] Julian 229C (*nosos*); 231D (*asebēmata*).

pagan worshippers is made abundantly clear. But the most striking moment in this work is the end, where Julian declares that the 'stain of atheism' must be removed.[9] The atheists, the godless ones, are of course the Christians; and again, as in the reply to Heracleius, Julian looks forward to their disappearance from his empire.

The letter about the murder of Bishop George of Cappadocia had indicated that Julian did not advocate illegality or open persecution as a means of wiping out the Christians. He preferred subtler means, especially inducements to recant and the purification of the younger generation. Advancement in the court and in the army could be made easier for pagans than for Christians. Later in 362 Julian wrote explicitly to a pagan governor, Atarbius, 'By the gods I do not want the Galilaeans to be killed or beaten unjustly nor to suffer any other ill. I do, however, state that the god-fearing (*theosebeis*) should be preferred to them. . . Honour should go to the gods and to the men and cities that worship them.'[10] This policy, so clearly enunciated here, may be traced back at least to the final months in Constantinople. It is fully consistent with Julian's writings at the time.

As to the purification of the young in the process of weakening the Christian establishment, Julian issued on 17 June 362 his notorious edict on teachers, an edict which even the admiring Ammianus judged deserving of everlasting silence.[11] At first reading, the edict seems innocuous; for Julian's words were carefully chosen: 'School teachers and professors ought to be distinguished, first by character and, second, by eloquence.' It was apparent that those who did not meet these qualifications were ineligible to teach the pagan texts which constituted the core of fourth-century education. Julian had a very high regard for learning, especially for rhetoric, in view of the impact of his own education in philosophy and rhetoric; and Libanius remarked after Julian's death that the emperor considered learning and religion to be intimately related and their fortunes intertwined.[12]

[9] Julian 180B (*tēs atheotētos tēn kēlīda*).
[10] Julian, *Lettres* (Bidez), no. 83 [376C–D].
[11] Amm. Marc. 22.10.7; 25.4.20.
[12] Libanius, *orat.* 18.157.

Hence when Julian issued his edict on teachers he was concerned as much with religion as with secular instruction. All of this comes clear in the explanatory letter which the emperor provided as an interpretation of his measure. No Christian, in his view, would qualify as a teacher because he was automatically deficient in character (*mores*).[13] Accordingly by a single stroke Julian forbade Christians to teach grammar, rhetoric, and philosophy. The cunningly oblique wording of the edict reflects the emperor's sincere conviction that no Christian who proposed to teach pagan classics could be a good person, for such a teacher would have to give instruction in something in which he did not believe. Julian did not think his edict unfair or his policy coercive. 'I am not telling such people [i.e. who teach the pagan classics] to change their mind. I am giving them a choice, either not to teach what they do not take seriously, or else to teach it as truth and to instruct the students accordingly.'[14]

By his educational policy Julian made the whole Hellenic tradition and its great literature the exclusive preserve of the pagans. Educated Christians, whose classical learning was palpably inferior to no one's, were confronted with the identification of Hellenism with paganism. Gregory of Nazianzus has left an eloquent protest against this appropriation by the pagans of a culture shared in common by Christians and pagan alike.[15] Julian knew perfectly well what he was doing. Within little more than a generation the educated élite of the empire would be pagan. The Christian intellectuals struggled to strike back and to set about the composition of a whole new literature to form the texts of a new Christian curriculum. Meanwhile, Julian announced that the Christians had to be cured of their disease like madmen, against their will. 'In my opinion,' he declared, 'one does not punish but instruct the insane.'[16] So if Julian tolerated the Christians in his

---

[13] Cod. Theod. XIII. 3.5: *Magistros studiorum doctoresque excellere oportet moribus primum, deinde facundia.* [14] Julian, *Lettres* (Bidez), no. 61 [423A].

[15] Greg. Naz., *orat.* 4.5, [Migne, *PG* 35.536A–B]. For the suggestion that the identification of Hellenism with paganism began with Iamblichus, see W. Koch, *Revue belge de philologie et d'histoire* 7 (1928), 539. It may well have begun even earlier with Porphyry, the teacher of Iamblichus.

[16] Julian, *Lettres* (Bidez), no. 61 [424B].

empire, it is easy to see what end he foresaw for them. He never contemplated any other solution to the religious problem than total elimination. His view of the Christians was utterly intolerant from the start.

Julian left Constantinople at about the time of the promulgation of his edict on teachers. He had already appointed his uncle, also called Julian and an enthusiastic convert to his nephew's faith, to the governorship of the East with a view, no doubt, to preparing for Julian's advent. The emperor was planning to go to the city of Antioch, with a large Christian population, as his base for launching a campaign against the Sassanian Persians. His uncle had much to do to revive pagan sentiments in a place that had grown so content with its own particularly ebullient brand of Christianity. Julian himself was to make his way eastward through Anatolia, visiting partisans and shrines. He had, it seemed, begun to formulate his plans for an integrated pagan church, with priests appointed by himself. He was to reintroduce the ancient and venerable title of *pontifex maximus* for the head of this church, the emperor.[17] From his youth Julian had realized the strength which Christianity derived from ecclesiastical organization.

The letters of Julian from the period of mid-June to mid-July when he was crossing Anatolia to Syrian Antioch show the zeal with which he endeavoured to stimulate the cause of paganism. A certain Pegasius he appointed a priest because years before, when a bishop, this same man had given Julian a tour of Troy. Julian had sensed in him even then a certain reverence for the gods and now that Pegasius had thrown over his Christian faith Julian judged him fit for a pagan priesthood (probably all the more so, as with his uncle Julian, because of the Christian past). In a surviving letter Julian defends his appointment of Pegasius with passionate conviction. To a certain Aristoxenus, who wanted an invitation to meet Julian, the emperor proposed that he find him at Tyana. Then he added, in an evangelical tone, 'Show us a man among the

[17] On Julian's organization of his church see W. Koch's important series of articles, 'Comment l'empereur Julien tâcha de fonder une église païenne', *Revue belge de philologie et d'histoire* 6 (1927), 123 ff.; 7 (1928), 49 ff.; 7 (1928), 511 ff.; 7 (1928), 1363 ff.

Cappadocians who is a pure Hellene.' (Again Hellenism in the religious sense.) 'For so far I have seen only those who do not wish to sacrifice, or else a few who want to but do not know how.'[18] The hectoring, insistent, wounded tone of this remark anticipates the subsequent disenchantment of the emperor with the recalcitrant Antiochenes and others who refused his demands.

Ritual and sacrifice were of paramount importance in the religion of Julian. Iamblichus and his followers had emphasized that the philosophic goal of a mystical union with the divine could only be achieved by ceremonial practices. Philosophy was inaccessible to most people, but its objectives were easily within the reach of those who performed rituals. Hence Julian's passionate devotion to the practice of cult. The little catechism of popular Neo-Platonism, *On the Gods and the World*, probably written by Julian's friend Salutius, is the best guide to the religion which Julian sought to establish in his empire.[18a] Spirits, demons, and angels were present in the world of the Neo-Platonists and could be drawn forth by theurgy—magic in the service of the gods. Sacrifice was an essential component of the ritual observances by which one approached the gods. Salutius wrote, 'Prayers divorced from sacrifices are only words, prayers with sacrifices are animated words.'

It was scarcely surprising that the recent author of an essay on the mother of the gods should have taken time on his passage through Anatolia to diverge from the route leading to Antioch so as to visit the shrine of the goddess at Pessinus. There he paid particular tribute to a faithful old priestess of Demeter named Callixena who had persevered in her duties despite the dangers that threatened under the rule of Constantine and his sons. Julian honoured the lady by appointing her to a priesthood of Cybele, for whose worship Pessinus was famous, in addition to the priesthood of Demeter, which she already held. In eulogizing Callixena Julian spoke of Pessinus as beloved of the gods.[19]

---

[18] Julian, *Lettres* (Bidez), no. 79 (on Pegasius); no. 78 [375C] (to Aristoxenus).
[18a] Cf. Appendix III below.
[19] Julian, *Lettres* (Bidez), no. 81 [388C–389A].

By the time the emperor had made his way through the Cilician Gates and on into Syria he began to receive the intelligence that his efforts to encourage the cults in Anatolia had not succeeded very well. The general situation as he had described it to Aristoxenus persisted. From Antioch he complained bitterly to Arsacius, the high priest of Galatia, about the failure of Hellenism—as Julian used the word; and he singled out for special censure the neglect of the mother of the gods at Pessinus.[20] Evidently the loyal Callixena was unable to do everything by herself. Julian threatened the people of Pessinus with imperial anger and surely repented of ever calling the place beloved of the gods. In reviewing the failure of his arrangements for the propagation of paganism, Julian determined to make more explicit the character of his new pagan church and the conduct of his priests. He endeavoured to imitate the most successful features of the Christian priesthood in his own church, to turn what he had learned as a youth to the greater glory of his gods.

'Do we not observe,' Julian asked the high priest of Galatia, 'that what has most of all fostered the growth of atheism (i.e. Christianity) is humanity (*philanthrōpia*) towards strangers, forethought in regard to the burial of the dead, and an affectation of dignity in one's life? Each of these ought, in my opinion, to be cultivated genuinely by us.'[21] Julian went on to instruct that his priests avoid theatres, taverns, and any occupations of ill-repute. He ordered that guest-houses be established in every city to give proof of the humanity (*philanthrōpia*) of the pagan priests. He provided for the free distribution of wheat and wine to the poor. The friends of Hellenism were to undertake this philanthropy and to wrest from the Galilaeans the credit they had earned from good works. Once more Julian's aim was the elimination of the impious Christians, but not by force or illegality. He did not want to give them martyrs. His Christian childhood had equipped him admirably for the struggle against his former coreligionists. Christians like Gregory of Nazianzus readily perceived what Julian was trying to do and fulminated against it.

[20] Julian, *Lettres* (Bidez), no. 84 [431D].   [21] Julian, *Lettres* (Bidez), no. 84 [429D].

It is evident that the humanitarian programme instituted by Julian was a calculated part of his scheme to wipe out the Christians rather than any reflection of a basic generosity of spirit on his own part. The letter to Arsacius the high priest is proof of this, and so is a fragmentary document of somewhat later date in which the emperor dilates at much greater length on the obligations of the pagan clergy. Here, in what appears to be a letter to a priest, Julian reiterated the importance of philanthropy as an expression of piety. He stressed the need for sacrifice and the value of adoring stone and wooden images of the gods. Julian demanded of priests as ascetic a way of life as his own. They were to avoid jests and obscenities, they were to read only edifying texts, they were forbidden to read erotic fiction, they were to wear plain attire in public, they were to stay away from theatrical performances and chariot-racing. And at the end Julian returned to the theme of humanitarianism to denounce the Christians for gaining credit by philanthropy. 'For just as those who entice children with a cake, and by throwing it to them two or three times induce them to follow them, and then, when they are far away from their friends cast them on board a ship and sell them as slaves, and that which for the moment seemed sweet, proves to be bitter for all the rest of their lives—by the same method, I say, the Galilaeans also begin with their so-called *agapē* and hospitality . . . and the result is that they have led very many into atheism.'[22]

When Julian composed that letter he had already tried still another means of unsettling and discrediting his Christian enemies. He had undertaken to rebuild the temple at Jerusalem— one of his most grandiose and celebrated projects. Although the move was naturally welcome to the Jews of Julian's empire and has given him a good reputation with Jews ever since, it would be wrong to consider it simply as an expression of friendly support for a people who had suffered so much under Roman rule. Some of Julian's writings betray a less than admiring disposition toward the Jews.[23] But Julian and the Jews had a common enemy in the

[22] Julian, *Lettres* (Bidez), no. 89 [305c].
[23] Cf. Julian, *Lettres* (Bidez), no. 111 [433A–c], and especially the *Contra Galilaeos* [e.g. 218B, 238B, 305E].

Christians; their allegiance could be valuable in the Near East, particularly in Mesopotamia where the emperor was going to conduct his campaign against the Persians. As *restaurator templorum*, the restorer of the temples,[24] Julian could hardly have missed the fact that the great temple of the Jews at Jerusalem had been in ruins since the days of Vespasian. Constantine and his mother, Helena, had given especial attention to turning Jerusalem into a Christian city through the building of churches and shrines. For over two hundred years Jews had been officially forbidden access to the site of their temple save on one day each year.[25]

Apart from a common hostility to the Christians, Julian was impelled to the Jewish cause by two major considerations. One was his recognition that the Jews had a tradition of offering sacrifices to their god, and throughout his empire he was doing his utmost to reinstitute the practice of sacrifice, without which—as the Neo-Platonist Iamblichus had declared—no prayer was complete.[26] Learning that the Jews could sacrifice, in accordance with their religion, only at the temple of Jerusalem, Julian had good reason to seek its restoration. The second consideration underlying Julian's enterprise was that the rebuilding of the temple would prove false the prophecy of Jesus that not one stone of the temple would be left upon another.[27] The falsification of this prophecy would constitute a blow to the credibility of the Christians.

While Julian appealed directly to the Jewish people to support his project and may have won their favour by the removal of taxes paid both to the Roman government and to the Jewish patriarch, it seems as if the court of the patriarch himself had some reason to be uneasy. Jews had been taught that the temple would be rebuilt only when the Messiah appeared, and it was therefore inappropriate for one who was both a Gentile and an idolater to initiate this work. Furthermore, the patriarch with his residence at

[24] See Appendix II below.

[25] By the fourth century this was evidently not enforced. There was even a synagogue in Jerusalem: M. Avi-Yonah, *The Jews of Palestine* (1976), p. 195.

[26] Cf. Avi-Yonah, op. cit., p. 187 and Iamblichus, *De Mysteriis*.

[27] Matthew 24.2; Mark 13.2; Luke 19.44 and 21.6. Ephraem, *Hymn against Julian* 4.20 cites Daniel (i.e. 9.26–7), rather than the New Testament, for the eternal desolation of the temple area.

Tiberias would naturally be superseded by the high priest in the restored temple at Jerusalem; and the House of Hillel, which provided the patriarchs, was not eligible to be transferred to the higher authority because it was not of priestly descent. An almost total silence in the Talmudic sources concerning Julian's plan may conceivably reflect a certain hesitation on the part of many rabbis in Palestine.[28]

Julian appointed Alypius, a former governor of Britain, to superintend the rebuilding project. But it did not go well. Before Julian left Antioch in early March of 363 and even before he wrote his long pastoral letter on the duties of the pagan clergy, the project had failed. According to Ammianus, great balls of fire burst out near the foundations of the temple and burned the construction workers.[29] This event, miraculous enough in the plain narrative of Ammianus, is more fantastically presented in the ecclesiastical historians who record fire from heaven, a mysterious cave, and frequent appearances of the Cross—in the sky, on clothing, on books, and on houses. The explanation of the troubles, whatever their exact form, may well have been an earthquake, which was and is a relatively common occurrence in that part of the world.[30] Sabotage in the form of an engineered miracle is also a possibility with a range of candidates, Christian and Jewish, who might have wished to terminate the project. In any case, the plan to rebuild the temple was abandoned.

In Egypt Julian found that his toleration edict had created a potentially dangerous situation for him, and from Antioch he sent instructions to the prefect Ecdicius.[31] Athanasius, the brilliant orthodox bishop who had been driven into hiding under the Arian emperor Constantius, had reappeared when Julian's policy of toleration was posted in Egypt in February of 362. Instead of devoting himself to quarrels with other Christians (as Julian had perhaps hoped), Athanasius made strenuous efforts to unite the Christians of the empire, and he proceeded to take up his episcopal position at Alexandria. His increasing popularity and influence

---

[28] Cf. Avi-Yonah, op. cit. (n. 25), p. 197.   [29] Amm. Marc. 23.1.3.
[30] See Appendix I below.   [31] Julian, *Lettres* (Bidez), no. 112 [376B–C].

there must have alarmed an emperor whose autocratic establishment of a pagan church had already encountered serious difficulties. Julian's strong sense of what was right combined with
indignation to produce a summary eviction of Athanasius from
his newly recovered position. The edict of toleration, Julian
explained to Ecdicius, did not mean that clergymen could return
to their churches, but only to their countries. It is unlikely that
Julian had planned to observe so subtle a distinction when he
initially issued his edict, but it is characteristic of the later months
of his reign that he was able to devise such sophistry to justify
steps he wanted taken. To the people of Alexandria Julian wrote,
'By the gods I feel much ashamed if any one of the Alexandrians
admits to being a Galilaean.'[32] And to Ecdicius he threatened
penalties if Athanasius were not out of Egypt by December of
362. In his own handwriting Julian added to the official letter to
Ecdicius that nothing would give him greater pleasure than to
know that Athanasius had been driven out, 'that accursed man
who has dared to baptize Greek women of good family in my
reign'. The outrage, the righteous indignation are tones which
became increasingly shrill in Julian's last months.

The pagan communities of several cities in the East took advantage of Julian's growing severity in the cause of exterminating the
Christians. Riots and massacres at Gaza, Emesa, and elsewhere
went virtually unpunished by the emperor and sometimes
praised.[33] In Cappadocia the emperor himself erased, as Libanius
put it, the city of Caesarea because the Christian element there had
prevailed over the pagan.[34] Julian's policies were edging close to
persecution. His more subtle arrangements to triumph over the
Christians had been far less successful than he had hoped, and
Athanasius, a worthy rival, had been heard to encourage his
friends by the remark that Julian's reign was just a little cloud
which would quickly pass.[35] So dismissive an attitude would have
infuriated the emperor.

[32] Julian, *Lettres* (Bidez), no. 111 [433A].
[33] Gaza: Greg. Naz. 4. 93 (Migne, *PG* 35. 625A–C); Sozomen 5.9. Emesa:
Julian, *Misop.* 357C.   [34] Libanius, *orat.* 16.14; Sozomen 5.4. 1 ff.
[35] *Historia acephala* 10; Sozomen 5.15.3.

Two of Julian's pastoral letters well illustrate his religious policies shortly before his departure on the Persian campaign in March, 363. In a letter to the Christians of Bostra, the capital of the province of Arabia, Julian formally denounced as criminals those who joined clergymen in anti-pagan demonstrations. He then mocked the claims of Titus, the bishop of Bostra, to have kept the mob in check. He twisted these claims into an accusation of bad character against the Christians of Bostra and incited them to drive out their own bishop from the city.[36] This is sophistry in the cause of sedition. To the northern Mesopotamian city of Edessa, once the seat of the Abgarid kings and an early centre of Syriac Christianity, Julian also addressed a letter. He asserted the gentleness and humanity of his treatment of the Christians in comparison with the savagery which the various opposing sects of Christians had shown to one another. Citing with bitter irony the Christian view that the poor will pass more easily to the Kingdom of Heaven than the rich, Julian summarily confiscated all the money and land of the Christian community of Edessa. He claimed thereby to improve their chances for admission to the heavenly kingdom.[37] Clever and cunning, Julian was now indisputably a persecutor.

As the emperor tightened his grip on the empire, he issued further restrictive legislation in support of his religious convictions. A recently discovered law of 17 January 363 seems to show that Julian was trying to eliminate Christians from the legal profession at Rome by confining their number to thirty and specifying that they be chosen on the basis of *animus* (spirit) and *facundia* (eloquence).[38] It is impossible to avoid the notion that *animus* here corresponds with *mores* (character) in the regulation of teachers and is a criterion by which Christians would be excluded. A month later, on 12 February, Julian proclaimed all daytime funerals illegal.[39] Strict Neo-Platonic doctrine, as given by

---

[36] Julian, *Lettres* (Bidez), no. 114 [435D–438C].
[37] Julian, *Lettres* (Bidez), no. 115 [424C–425A].
[38] B. Bischoff—D. Nörr, *Bayerische Akad. der Wiss.*, Phil.–Hist. Klasse, Abh., N. F. 58 (1963).
[39] Cod. Theod. IX. 17.5. Cf. Julian, *Lettres* (Bidez), no. 136b.

Iamblichus, condemned the sight of a corpse in daytime as a defilement; for the dead belonged to the infernal gods of the night. But Julian had not been disconcerted in late 361 when he joined in the obsequies for Constantius. Fanaticism feeds on itself, and the author of the letters to Alexandria, Bostra, and Edessa might be expected to have become more rigorous in those religious observances to which he would expect everyone to conform. He had become obsessed by purificatory rites. He had had removed the corpses buried near the Castalian spring at Delphi, he had had the corpses of martyrs near the temple at Didyma burned, he had eulogized the people of Emesa for burning Christian tombs, and at Daphne near Antioch he had had the remains of the martyr Babylas removed to revive the oracle of Apollo.[40]

Indications of the pagan revival appear on some inscriptions in praise of Julian as well as on eastern milestones proclaiming 'One Julian' in place of the Christian formula 'One God'.[41] And at Syrian Apamea, a mosaic seems to show the emperor in the role of a latter-day Socrates.[42] But overall the revival was in trouble, and nowhere more visibly than in the lively and populous city where Julian resided from July of 362 until his departure against the Persians in March of the next year. Antioch was no place for a puritanical pagan.

[40] Amm. Marc. 22.12.8 (Delphi); Sozomen 5.20.7 (Didyma); Julian, *Misop.* 357c (Emesa); for Babylas see the following chapter.
[41] R. Brünnow and A. von Domaszewski, *Die Provincia Arabia* vol. 2 (1905), pp. 232–3 (near Jerash).
[42] J. Balty and J. Ch. Balty, *Annales Univ. Besançon* 166 (1974), 267 ff. Cf. p. 19 above.

CHAPTER NINE

Antioch

BY the waters of the River Orontes and beneath the slopes of Mt. Casius Antioch was, in the fourth century, the most populous and exciting city of the Near East. With easy access to the sea at its port of Seleuceia and linked with the desert by way of Beroea (modern Aleppo), it was ideally suited to emperors who contemplated campaigning further east. The city was marvellously cosmopolitan, with its fusion of Hellenism and an indigenous Semitic culture. While the inhabitants were predominantly Christian, pagan traditions were well represented by Libanius and other intellectuals; and the Christian style of life had an old-fashioned pagan zest to it. There was a substantial Jewish settlement, subject to the patriarch at Tiberias and on reasonably good terms with its neighbours. The Antiochenes were a spirited people, keen on theatre and chariot-racing; their city boasted Olympic games, which were only less prestigious than those at Olympia itself and eagerly sought out by the professional athletes of the age. Outside the city lay a fertile countryside of largely Syriac culture. Even Libanius knew some Syriac and was doubtless not the only Hellenic purist who was able to draw information and inspiration from native traditions. In the streets of Antioch, with its colonnades and mosaics, the soldiers, scholars, shopkeepers, and perhaps even saints thrived in this invigorating polyglot community.

When the news of Constantius' death reached Antioch, there was, according to Libanius,[1] great rejoicing, although not perhaps to the degree the sophist tried to suggest. Yet Antioch was certainly glad to welcome the new emperor, and an embassy, no

[1] Libanius, *orat.* 15. 48.

doubt representing the city council—or curia, went to greet Julian at Constantinople. Julian was later to complain peevishly that the Antiochene embassy was the last to arrive in Constantinople, but it is clear from his response at that time that he had found no fault with the city. On the contrary, he immediately took steps to ease the economic difficulties of which he must have been advised by the ambassadors. As in most Greek cities, the financial burdens of Antioch devolved upon the members of the curia, but they were too few in number and often insufficiently affluent to meet the demands. And the situation had been recently exacerbated by a drought which imperilled the next harvest. Julian promptly cancelled the city's arrears of taxes, and he added two hundred more places to the curia in the hope of enrolling more men of substance to contribute to civic financing. He had still more elaborate plans for improving and ennobling Antioch: 'I was planning to make your city greater and more powerful.'[2]

In choosing Antioch as the imperial headquarters after his departure from Constantinople, Julian was undoubtedly thinking in the first instance of an appropriate base from which to launch his projected campaign against the Persians. Constantius had conducted his military operations from the same place, and Julian would be taking with him as many of Constantius' men as he could trust in addition to the troops he had brought with him from Gaul. Antioch was the obvious place. Yet Julian may, in the beginning, have hoped to find more there than simply a military base. The city had had a distinguished Hellenic past since its origins under the first Seleucid king. There were shrines and temples, as well as the famous oracle of Apollo at Daphne on the outskirts of Antioch. Libanius, whom Julian had admired from his boyhood, was a respected teacher in the city. When Julian once told Libanius, with a clear reminiscence of Augustus' celebrated remark about Rome, that he intended to make Antioch a city of marble, he perhaps implied that he envisaged a grander role for the city in the future than that of headquarters for eastern

[2] Julian, *Misop.* 367D.

operations.[3] He may have seen in Antioch a new seat of empire. Whatever Julian may have had in mind, troubles began from the day of his arrival on 18 July 362. A crowd that welcomed him shouted that a salubrious star had shone upon the East, but the goodwill of that delegation was seriously offset by the sound of wailing and lamentation that rose from the streets and houses of the city.[4] It was the annual celebration of the Adonia, when the death of Venus' beloved Adonis was mourned. This pagan observance had persisted in the largely Christian city as one of its many holidays, and that Julian entered engulfed by levantine ululations was scarcely a good omen.

Soon after his arrival Julian appeared in the hippodrome before a large throng of the Antiochene people. They made a great clamour with their cries that everything was plentiful in the city but expensive.[5] A famine was breaking out because of the sharp business practices of the rich, who were apparently guilty of hoarding and selling at high prices. Inflation was nothing new at Antioch and was more attributable to the regular presence of an army in recent years than to the drought of the preceding winter. Julian at first imagined that the economic situation could be left to the care of the curia with its two hundred additional members. He conferred with the leading citizens and tried to persuade them, rather unrealistically, to despise unjust profits. They agreed to look after the problem. The emperor's deliberate policy of strengthening local councils and giving them greater autonomy was reflected in the honorific title he was given, *curiarum et rei publicae recreator* (reviver of the councils and the state).[6] Leaving the famine issue in the hands of the revived curia of Antioch, Julian felt free to attend to other matters. His own strict standards of personal propriety made it impossible for him to comprehend now—or ever—the daily corruption and confusion in which many cities muddle through, and often achieve brilliance. The curia of Antioch was to disappoint him gravely.

[3] Libanius, *orat.* 15.52. Cf. Suetonius, *Aug.* 28.
[4] Amm. Marc. 22.9.15.
[5] Julian, *Misop.* 368D: they chanted *panta gemei, panta pollou.*
[6] See Appendix II below.

It was only to be expected that Julian's principal concerns at Antioch would be with Hellenism in both the cultural and religious senses. He sought out Libanius who had waited for the emperor to make the first move. Libanius acted from a proper sense of his own dignity and station (and possibly a recollection of the similar way in which the great second-century sophist Aristides had behaved toward Marcus Aurelius).[7] Julian also visited the temples and shrines of the city, and he was eager to perform sacrifices. He worshipped at the altars of Zeus, Tyche, Demeter, Hermes, Apollo and others; and for convenience he worshipped as well within the confines of the imperial palace.[8] A few weeks after his arrival in Antioch he went out to the shrine of Apollo at Daphne, 'thinking', as he wrote later, 'that at Daphne, if anywhere, I should enjoy the sight of your wealth and public spirit'.[9] He pictured to himself the sacrificial animals, libations, and choruses for the annual festival of the god, but when he got there he found nothing prepared. As pontifex maximus he thought that perhaps he was expected to give some signal to start the proceedings, but when he made inquiry of the local priest he learned that the city was about to do nothing. The priest had brought a goose from his house to provide the sole sacrifice to the god.

Outraged by this experience, Julian berated the members of the curia.[10] He denounced their private luxury and their neglect of the gods, and he thereby won himself no friends. The good life of the Antiochenes had no appeal for the ascetic monarch, and his piety had no appeal for them. He made known his disapproval of theatrical performances and chariot-racing, and he refused to witness either. The process of alienation was underway. Mutual hatred was to come.

Meanwhile Julian watched with concern the deteriorating economic situation. On 18 August he ruled that military rations were to be drawn only by those officers actually instructed to be

[7] Cf. R. Pack, *Classical Philology* 42 (1947), 17 ff.
[8] Julian, *Misop.* 346B–D; Libanius, *orat.* 1.121–2 and 15.79.
[9] Julian, *Misop.* 361D.
[10] Julian, *Misop.* 362B–363C.

on duty at court.[11] Supernumerary officers also drawing rations were discharged and obliged to go home. This measure was unlikely to have made a great difference to the food supply, but it was very much in character for Julian to impose austerity upon his troops as a model for the Antiochenes. They, however, would not have been likely to view the matter in this way. For Julian's enthusiasm to renew sacrifices had led to some ugly scenes in which the pagan soldiers, stuffed with sacrificial meat and flown with wine, made a public nuisance of themselves. Julian, firm in his convictions, was blind to the problem of the soldiers after sacrifice and went out of his way to give support to the most unruly of them—the faithful units of Celts and Petulantes from Gaul.[12]

As time passed, it became increasingly apparent that Julian's naïve expectation of refreshing the curia was not being fulfilled. To enlarge the pool of candidates for service Julian announced on 28 August that eligibility could pass through the female line as well as the male. A short time afterward (3 September) he permitted the enrolment of local residents with curial status in other cities.[13] But this was all unavailing. The burden of service in the curia was such that persons of affluence did their best to stay out of it and because of their affluence were often successful in doing so. Julian discovered that his best efforts to secure the recruitment of useful new councillors were being systematically frustrated by the nomination of poor and unqualified candidates. Poor souls from the market-place were dragged in and, with the offer of a modest bribe which seemed a fortune, persuaded to join the curia. On 18 September in an edict to the praetorian prefect of the East Julian abruptly and testily declared all the recent nominations to councils invalid and ordered a formal investigation of the preceding nominations.[14] This drastic readjustment of his plan to enlarge the curiae was evidently the direct outcome of the corruption he observed at Antioch. The relations between him and the leaders of the city deteriorated further.

---

[11] Cod. Theod. VI. 24.1.   [12] Amm. Marc. 22.12.6. Cf. Julian, *Misop.* 342A.
[13] Cod. Theod. XII. 1.51. (Aug. 28); Cod. Theod. XII. 1.52 (Sept. 3).
[14] Cod. Theod. XII. 1.53.

At Daphne Julian had wanted to consult the oracle of Apollo near the Castalian spring not far from the god's temple, but he discovered that the oracle had been silenced by none other than his notorious brother, Gallus, while serving as Caesar in the East. Gallus, a zealous Christian, had ordered that the earthly remains of an eminent Antiochene martyr, St. Babylas, be transferred from their resting-place in the city to the vicinity of the temple and spring at Daphne. Julian was informed by the custodians of the temple that the oracle was now silent because there were bodies in the vicinity. Judging this explanation to be an allusion to the remains of Babylas, the emperor had the place ritually purified, and the saint's bones taken back to their original grave. A crowd of jubilant Christians, rejoicing in so palpable a proof of the power of their martyr, accompanied the coffin to the city with exultant singing. Shortly thereafter, on 22 October, the temple of Apollo burned. Both the roof and the huge chryselephantine statue of the god were destroyed. The cause of the blaze was unknown, but suspicion fell upon the Christians. They themselves offered lightning as their explanation, while there was also a rumour that sparks from candles lit by a pagan philosopher worshipping at the temple had started the fire.[15]

In a fury Julian ordered an investigation and authorized a severity greater than usual—presumably torture. He closed the great octagonal Church of Antioch and confiscated its liturgical vessels.[16] His display of righteous indignation terminated any hope he may have had of peacefully persuading the Christians of the city to abandon their faith, and with the already strained relations he had with the council the possibility of turning Antioch into an imperial city became very remote. In a desperate attempt to salvage what goodwill might remain the emperor curried favour directly with the people by personal intervention to relieve the famine. In refusing any longer to recognize the council's responsibility in this matter, Julian incurred sharp criticism from Ammianus,

---

[15] Amm. Marc. 22.13.1–3.
[16] Theodoret 3.12.4. See G. Downey, *A History of Antioch in Syria* (1961), p. 388 with n. 48.

himself an Antiochene, for courting popularity. It seems more than likely that Julian was trying to rescue himself from a serious crisis by exploiting the famine; yet, for all that, he cannot be accused of hypocrisy or insincerity. He believed that everything he had done was right; he had no need—nor the temperament—to apologize, but he also believed that the Christians should not have a monopoly in humanitarian assistance. It was perfectly consistent with his own pastoral instructions to the priests of the pagan church that the supreme pontiff should himself take steps to feed the poor.

Recognizing that most commodities except grain were not in short supply but simply overpriced through the profiteering of the wealthy, Julian established fixed prices for everything.[17] The drought had reduced the available quantity of grain, and to meet this shortage he imported large amounts first from the cities of Chalcis and Hierapolis in Syria, then from imperial properties in the province, and ultimately from Egypt. And he set a price well below that which had been current.[18] Since Julian did not provide for rationing of the grain which he made available and furthermore did nothing to control the prices of commodities outside the city, the clever rich of Antioch easily managed to make a profit from the emperor's naïve measures. They bought up the grain at the cheap price and sold it in the countryside at a high price along with oil, wine, and other items. Julian imposed controls on the prices asked by the bakers for their bread, and since bread is not easily hoarded it became the only thing in Antioch that was both plentiful and cheap.[19] Country residents poured into the city to buy it and returned home to pay artificially high prices for other commodities which could not be found in the city. Meanwhile to resettle some of the urban poor and to encourage greater production of foodstuffs Julian made three thousand lots of municipal land available for cultivation, but he made no provision to prevent the wealthy landowners from simply adding this to their properties.[20] Julian's effort to relieve

[17] Julian, *Misop.* 368D–369A.   [18] Julian, *Misop.* 369A–B.
[19] Julian, *Misop.* 369D.   [20] Julian, *Misop.* 370D.

the economic crisis was a disaster. Apart from Libanius and perhaps a few others like him, Julian had few friends left in Antioch.

His sojourn there was proving a failure, and he was far too intelligent not to realize this. He found himself alienated from both the populace and the aristocracy; he viewed the Christians of Antioch with unremitting rage. The Hellenism of the city was a perfectly genuine form of Hellenism, but it was not his; and that made all the difference. Julian was not about to give up the great programme to which he had dedicated himself. He was altogether incapable of changing his character, of relaxing in the theatre or the hippodrome with a lively mob, of discovering sex after a total abstinence of seven years. His consciousness of failure drove him to write a series of pieces in which he released all his frustrations.

During the riotous festival of the Saturnalia from 15 to 17 December 362, Julian seized the opportunity to compose a satirical dialogue on his predecessors as emperors of the Roman world. The work, commonly known as the *Caesars*, gave ample scope to Julian's irony and bitterness.[21] Its review of the emperors, one by one, represents an attempt to place his own reign in some kind of perspective, and inevitably it is most valuable for what it reveals of the ideals and prejudices of its author. His identification of himself with Alexander the Great and with Marcus Aurelius is easily discernible from the treatment each receives, and—in the case of Alexander—from the very fact that he is included at all. The authentic voice of Julian can be heard in the speech he assigned to Alexander at the imaginary banquet of the emperors: 'If some things I did seemed cruel I never was so to the innocent but only to those who had often and in many ways thwarted me and had made no proper or fitting use of their opportunities.'[22] And again when Marcus Aurelius is made to

---

[21] It is probably best to assume that the *Kronia* mentioned at 157c in Julian's discourse on the Sun is identical with the extant *Caesars*, which is named in the manuscripts *sumposion ē Kronia*. The Souda lexicon, however, cites two distinct works, *Caesars* and *Kronia*.

[22] Julian, *Caesars* 325B. Cf. p. 16 above.

explain his ideal of 'imitating the gods', it is Julian's asceticism that underlies the response of Marcus: 'Having the fewest possible needs and doing good to the greatest possible number.' When asked if he had had no needs at all, Marcus replied, 'I had none, but my wretched body had perhaps a few.'[23] Julian's attitude to the Christians is more than suggested by his treatment of Constantine at the end. Anger breaks through as Constantine is depicted in the arms of Pleasure, who introduces him to Incontinence. Cohabiting with Incontinence is Jesus, crying aloud: 'He that is a seducer, he that is a murderer, he that is sacrilegious and infamous, let him approach without fear. For with this water I will wash him and immediately make him clean.'[24]

It appears that it was also during this same period that Julian was at work on another project, which may well have continued to occupy him down to the end of his stay at Antioch. This was the tractate, now lost, 'Against the Galilaeans', in which the emperor undertook a full-scale assault on the doctrines of Christianity and the conduct of its adherents. We can form some notion of the work from the extensive critique of it by Cyril of Alexandria in the fifth century.[25] Julian made good use of the learning of his childhood to produce citations from the Old and New Testaments. He argued at length from contradictions and discrepancies he discovered that the Christians had no consistent theology. Moreover, he charged them with unwarranted innovations like the cult of martyrs, and he accused them of hypocrisy for preaching universal love while condemning heretics. The work on the Galilaeans was a systematically argued complement to the satire of the *Caesars*. By turning to the written word, Julian was resorting to a form of expression of which he knew he was a master and which might have an influence without obliging him to enter further into personal relations with anyone.

The increasing isolation of the emperor at Antioch seems also to be the background of another of his surviving writings, although the work is so personal and intense that it is difficult to

---

[23] Julian, *Caesars* 334A.   [24] Julian, *Caesars* 336A–B.
[25] Cf. R. Asmus, *Julians Galiläerschrift* (1904).

be certain of the year of composition. It is the discourse to Helios
the king on the occasion of the celebration of *Sol Invictus* on 25
December. It is a sustained utterance of great piety in tribute to
the sun—not merely the visible sun but the sun as a transcendent
mediating force between the Neo-Platonic One and the intelligible
world. A reference toward the end to a recently composed work
for the Saturnalia makes it probable that this discourse belongs
to late December of 362, in the days immediately following the
Caesars.[26] If so, it is a striking document of the inwardness and
religiosity with which Julian sought refreshment from the vexations of Antioch.

Those vexations grew worse in the early months of 363. The
people of the city directed lampoons and satires at Julian. They
made fun of his beard and derided his austere style of life. Two of
his close advisers had recently died, Felix, a high financial officer
of Neo-Platonic persuasion, and his uncle Julian. The latter died
from a particularly grisly and painful disease that afforded great
pleasure to the emperor's Christian enemies, who saw in this the
vengeance of God.[27] The people of Antioch thought back
nostalgically to life under the Arian Constantine, and they were
heard to say that neither Chi nor Kappa ever wronged their city.
By these letters they referred to the first letter of the names in
Greek of Christ and Constantius.[28] Julian's indignation over-
flowed and once again found expression in the medium he controlled best, the written word. He issued an impassioned reply,
the *Misopogon* or 'Beard-Hater'.

Julian intended this work to be ironic, detached, scathing in its
wit. He wanted to mock himself in a way that would demonstrate
the folly of his enemies and his own integrity. He poured scorn on
the Antiochenes' remarks about his beard and his way of life by
carrying their taunts to absurdity. The opening pages of the
Misopogon are at times genuinely amusing even where the self-
righteousness of the author becomes uncomfortably obvious.

[26] This dating presupposes that Julian wrote only one work entitled *Kronia*,
and that it is the extant work we call the *Caesars*. See note 21 above.
[27] Ephraem, *Hymn against Julian* 4.3; cf. Theodoret 3.9; Sozomen 5.8.
[28] Julian, *Misop.* 357A.

But Julian was unable to keep up the tone he had adopted. His wrath was too great. He felt thwarted, and, as he had made Alexander the Great observe, being thwarted was intolerable. A hectoring, injured, repetitive tone comes to dominate the *Misopogon*, and his cry at the end is that memorable cry of an outraged and helpless man: 'Why, in the name of the gods, are you ungrateful to me? Because I fed you from my own resources . . .?'[29] Ingratitude is the theme of the *Misopogon*.

As the day of his departure for Mesopotamia approached, Julian's rage was savage and threatening. To serve in his place at Antioch he appointed a man he knew to be cruel, one Alexander of Heliopolis. Julian commented that while Alexander did not deserve the appointment he was the right person to control the greedy and insulting people of Antioch.[30] Furthermore Julian announced that he had no intention of ever returning to that city after his campaign: he would take up residence at Tarsus instead.[31] About this time he also seems to have caused the issue of a new coin type, unexplained to this day but very probably having some kind of personal or mystical significance for the emperor. It showed a bull with two stars. In proclaiming in rich Syriac verse that this was the golden calf, Ephraem at Edessa only proved that the meaning of Julian's strange new coinage was quite unknown even then.[32]

As Julian left Antioch a crowd of citizens accompanied him in the hope of softening his anger. For it had gradually become obvious to the more perceptive Antiochenes that Julian's displeasure would have very serious consequences for their city. They could recall the near annihilation he had inflicted upon Caesarea in Cappadocia, and they will not have been ignorant of his increasingly autocratic treatment of places like Alexandria, Bostra, or Edessa. Libanius, in two discourses from this anxious time, eloquently showed his concern, or rather his fear. Although the speeches were never actually delivered owing to the rapid and

[29] Julian, *Misop.* 370c.   [30] Amm. Marc. 23.2.3.

[31] Libanius, *orat.* 15.77; 16.53.

[32] Ephraem, *Hymn against Julian* 16–19. On the coinage (but without knowledge of Ephraem), F. D. Gilliard, *Journal of Roman Studies* 54 (1964), 138 ff.

decisive course of events, a sense of urgency and alarm permeates the surviving texts. One was addressed to Julian after his initial successes on campaign, the other to the citizens of Antioch.[33]

With Julian Libanius pleaded for pardon, reminded him of his original plan to make the city great, and called his attention to the many shrines at which he had sacrificed. Libanius cited the emperor's benefactions as proof that he must, in his heart, care for the city. 'Must we be punished then? My lord, we have been punished already ... We hate ourselves, our soil, our climate, our waters, our homes and all who meet us. We avoid each other's company.'[34] To his fellow citizens Libanius adopted a tone less abject and more realistic. Julian was not like most men, he advised them: 'he has more control over his lower appetites than over the cities he rules'.[35] The way to survival lay in repentance and change. Close the theatre, reduce the number of chariot races. Libanius argued that self-punishment would be easier to bear than any the emperor would impose. The citizens should give up their Christianity and return to the temples. 'Shall we not persuade people to go there,' asked Libanius, 'or drag them by main force?'[36]

[33] Libanius, *orat.* 15 and 16.
[35] Libanius, *orat.* 16.18.
[34] Libanius, *orat.* 15.73.
[36] Libanius, *orat.* 16.56.

CHAPTER TEN

The Final Campaign

LIKE Alexander the Great, Julian had turned his eyes irrevocably to the East. He had gone to Antioch to prepare for a campaign against the Persians, who had for so long menaced the armies of Constantius. The failure of his policies in that city must have made him all the more determined to leave it. In feeding his anger, the troubles at Antioch had weakened his judgment. He would return triumphant, vindicated. He had never known a serious military defeat and would have found such a thing unimaginable. When the Persians, who viewed Julian's presence at Antioch with understandable concern, offered to send an embassy empowered to work out a peaceful settlement, the emperor rejected the proposal at once. An embassy was unnecessary: the Persians would be seeing him soon.[1]

But Julian's confidence was not altogether justified. His relations with the army were still uneasy, and the concessions he had made to the military at the funeral of Constantius and at the Chalcedon trials had by no means removed the tension and suspicion. In particular, the eastern troops of Constantius had been demoralized by defeat at the hands of the Persians, and their military discipline left much to be desired. Moreover, they were predominantly Christian. It was Julian's deliberate policy to convert them to the worship of the pagan gods, and when necessary he was prepared to bribe them to this end. As Libanius declared, 'His actions were designed to secure their active support: he induced the hand that was going to grasp the spear to grasp offerings of incense and

[1] Libanius, *orat.* 18.164. Cf. Amm. Marc. 22.12.1, on Julian's desire to avenge Roman misfortunes in the East: *ad ultionem praeteritorum vehementer elatus est.*

6. Gold coin of Julian (reverse with legionary dragging captive: *Virtus exercitus Romanorum*). Mint of Antioch.

libation, so that they would be able to pray, when the weapons were flying, to those who had it in their power to check them. If persuasion proved insufficient, gold and silver co-operated to ensure adherence, and through this petty profit the soldiery secured a greater gain: by accepting a piece of gold, they won the friendship of the gods, the lords of war.'[2] Christian observers viewed this purification of the troops with less sympathy and commemorated those who resisted the emperor's solicitations.

The Church gained martyrs through Julian's zeal. Two standard-bearers of the important units which had attended the proceedings at Chalcedon, the Joviani and Herculiani, stubbornly refused to follow the imperial order to remove the Christian symbol, the *labarum*, from their standards; and they refused to perform sacrifices to the pagan gods. After a scrutiny by Julian's uncle, they were beheaded. This happened late in 362 or early in the next year.[3] At about the same time, two other officers were exiled for plans which Ammianus describes by the vague but sinister phrase 'beyond their capacity'.[4] Those men came from the *scutarii* in the emperor's own guard, as did two more who were reported for inflammatory comments and subsequently executed. Libanius provides unimpeachable evidence of a conspiracy to assassinate Julian.[5]

Yet it was not only the Christians who were restless and recalcitrant in the months just before the emperor launched his final campaign. His own fellow pagans mounted opposition in terms which it was difficult for Julian to ignore. It was suggested that the gods themselves advised against the campaign. In January of 363, the officer Felix died, in the company of Julian, from a sudden haemorrhage; a priest suddenly dropped dead on the steps of the temple of Genius; there was an earthquake at Constantinople; the Sibylline Books, consulted at Rome on the

---

[2] Libanius, *orat.* 18.168.

[3] The martyrs were Bonosus and Maximilianus: *Acta sanctorum* (Paris, 1867), IV. 430 ff.; cf. Ruinart, *Acta sincera*, pp. 592–3. See also B. de Gaiffier, *Analecta Bollandiana* 74 (1956), 9 f.

[4] Romanus and Vincentius: Amm. Marc. 22.11.2 (*quaedam suis viribus altiora*).

[5] Juventinus and Maximinus: Theodoret 3.15.4–9; John Chrysostom, *PG* (Migne) 50.571–578. Cf. Libanius, *orat.* 18.199.

prospects for Julian's war, unambiguously instructed him to desist.[6] The interpreters of omens were agreed that Julian should not go. All these edifying details are scrupulously recorded by Ammianus, and they contribute to the impression that there was an increasing resistance to Julian's megalomania on the part of the pagans themselves.

The unpleasant position in which the emperor found himself at Antioch may have strengthened Julian's resolve to pay no heed to the admonitions of pagan exegetes and to take no warning from the disturbances in his army. On 5 March 363, he went out from Antioch on his ill-omened mission with a force of some eighty to ninety thousand men. The wiser of the Antiochenes may have recalled that in the preceding September Julian had published an edict that affirmed, 'Military service is of the first importance in the state. Next is the embellishment of peace through the protection of literature.'[7] With these priorities Julian left Libanius behind at Antioch. It would be interesting to know whether or not the emperor's literary intimates, like the rhetorician Libanius or the Neo-Platonist Maximus, attempted to dissuade him from the Persian enterprise. While Libanius remained in the city and endeavoured to reconcile its citizens to Julian by frightening them with the consequences of his wrath, Maximus, along with Priscus and Oribasius, joined in the expedition. It is possible that their Neo-Platonic sensibilities had not been affected by the omens of a more traditional paganism, or rather that they were able to put Julian's anxieties to rest. Julian's religious fanaticism had been genuine and sincere. If his ambition now led him to disregard the signs from the gods, he was probably reassured by those few spiritual counsellors on whom he had so long depended.

Having proudly rejected offers of assistance from various peoples, Julian instructed only Arsaces, the king of Armenia, to make provision for him and to supply additional forces.[8] The first days of the expedition were passed in Syria, as the army made its way to Beroea (modern Aleppo) by way of the outskirts

---

[6] Amm. Marc. 23.1.5–7. Cf. D. Conduché, *Latomus* 24 (1965), 368.
[7] Cod. Theod. VI. 26.1. [8] Amm. Marc. 23.2.2.

of Chalcis, and on to Syrian Batnae and Hierapolis. Julian
wrote to Libanius a letter giving his impressions and noting
especially the devotion, or lack of it, to the pagan gods.[9] At
Beroea Zeus provided a clear omen of success to the emperor, who
sacrificed a white bull to the god on the acropolis of the city.
While the councillors of Beroea listened politely to Julian as he
lectured them on piety, he had to confess to Libanius that he
managed to persuade only those few men who had already been
persuaded before he spoke but were too cautious to admit it. The
timidity and complaisance of human kind moved him to expostu-
late bitterly on the lack of courage and piety. At Batnae a different experience awaited him—ostentatious sacrificing, no doubt
in a vain hope of winning his favour. But again Julian protested.
The pious pagan should not call attention to himself in his
worship.

Five days after his departure Julian reached Hierapolis, where
he made contact with Arabs of the desert who wished to serve in
his army. He saw to the preparation of supplies and received
news of the fleet that was being organized on the Euphrates
further north.[10] It is clear that his plan at this stage was to march
south along the river into southern Mesopotamia.

Before doing this, however, he took his troops directly across
the Euphrates into northern Mesopotamia. By this feint he
suggested a different approach to the Persian kingdom from the
one he actually had in mind, and he could also visit the celebrated
temple of the Moon at Carrhae. There was a rumour that when
he stood before the altar with an obscure kinsman by the name of
Procopius and no one else present, he turned over to this man a
purple cloak and instructed him to seize power if he should perish
among the Persians.[11] Although Ammianus duly reports this
gossip, it may only reflect Procopius' unsuccessful attempt to
become emperor two years later. Ammianus is more concerned
to suggest that Julian had begun at last to realize that he was on a

[9] Julian, *Lettres* (Bidez), no. 98 [399B–402B].
[10] ibid. [402A].
[11] Amm. Marc. 23.3.2. Cf. J. Béranger, *Bonner Historia–Augusta–Colloquium*
1970 (1972), pp. 88–9, n. 57.

fatal mission. He was tormented by dreams at Carrhae on—as it was learned later—the very night on which the temple of Palatine Apollo at Rome was consumed by fire.[12]

But Julian went on. He directed that Procopius and the former *dux* of Egypt, Sebastianus, lead some thirty thousand men eastward to devastate Media with the help of the troops from the Armenian king. After this diversionary action they were to march south to join Julian and his army in the vicinity of Ctesiphon. Meanwhile, after a pretence of heading toward the Tigris, Julian veered round and marched to the Euphrates.[13] He reached the river at Callinicum (modern Raqqa), and there on 27 March he celebrated with joy and solemnity the rites of the mother of the gods, for whose worship his extant treatise proves his exceptional regard. Shortly thereafter he was greeted by some local Arab sheikhs and presented with a golden crown. Meanwhile the fleet which had been prepared for him arrived on the river. One thousand ships were laden with supplies, weapons, and siege-works, and they were accompanied by fifty war-ships and an equal number of flat-bottom boats to effect the bridging of rivers when necessary. Together with the Arab reinforcements, Julian's army, still in Roman territory, moved southward to the confluence of the river Khabūr with the Euphrates at Circesium. Here a bridge of ships was set up to permit the troops to cross over the Khabūr. As Julian was supervising these operations, a letter reached him from his trusted prefect of the Gauls, Sallustius, who implored him to give up the expedition. It was untimely, Sallustius wrote; and if he persevered the gods would deliver him to death.[14] The emperor chose to ignore this advice and pressed on. Once the army had crossed the Khabūr and left Roman territory behind them, Julian had the bridge removed so that no one would think of turning back.

Another omen portended disaster. The corpse of a provisions officer, who had been condemned by Salutius the prefect and executed, was discovered, perhaps washed up on the shore of the Euphrates. The army next passed the tomb of Gordian III who

[12] Amm. Marc. 23.3.3.   [13] Amm. Marc. 23.3.5–6.   [14] Amm. Marc. 23.5.4.

8. Gold coin of Julian (reverse with variant type of legionary dragging captive: *Virtus exercitus Romanorum*). Mint of Antioch.

9. Two examples, obverse and reverse, of Julian's bronze coinage depicting a bull. Mints of Antioch and Arles, with reverse legend *Securitas rei pub(licae)*. Socrates 3.17 and Sozomen 5.19 mention Julianic coins depicting a bull to be sacrificed on an altar, but no such type has been found. It is probably a Christian fabrication based on inexact reports of the real bull coinage.

had perished on his campaign against the Persians, and it then passed opposite the deserted city of Dura-Europus, high above the river on its west bank. There a huge lion was slain, a portent which foretold the death of a king. The soothsayers in Julian's train were indignant that their admonitions against the war were so little credited, and they brought out their books to prove their point. But, says Ammianus, it was the philosophers who rejected their opinions: these enjoyed great authority, but persevered in matters about which they were ill-informed.[15] The influence of Maximus, Priscus, and Oribasius must have been decisive in Julian's camp, but opposition among the pagan soldiery could not be avoided for long.

In early April, as the sun was setting a menacing clap of thunder was followed by a flash of lightning which struck a soldier called Jovian. The soothsayers again pressed Julian to turn back, and again Ammianus declares that it was the philosophers who made nothing of their views.[16] The expedition advanced further into Persian territory.

Keeping the Euphrates on their right, the forces spread themselves over a substantial distance so as to appear even more numerous and formidable than they were. In the centre of the vast moving column was Julian with infantry. On the right, alongside the river, Nevitta commanded two legions; and on the left Arinthaeus and a renegade Persian, Hormizdas, guided the cavalry. Dagalaifus, Victor, and Secundinus, the *dux* of Osrhoene, were the commanders of the columns in the rear. At the front was Lucillianus, the master of the infantry. And on the river itself were over a thousand ships. It was only to be expected that, confronted with such a force, the inhabitants of Anatha, a fortified island in the Euphrates, should have surrendered and permitted themselves to be resettled in Syrian Chalcis. At the next fortified place, Thilutha, the emperor accepted the promise of the residents to support whoever emerged as victor in the coming war. As

[15] Amm. Marc. 23.5.6 (corpse); 23.5.8 (lion); 23.5.10–11 (soothsayers vs. philosophers).
[16] Amm. Marc. 23.5.12–14. Julian's successor as emperor was, of course, named Jovian.

the army went on, it passed by more towns with exotic names—
Achaiachala, Baraxmalcha, Ozogardana; and it saw the remains
of abandoned forts as well as reminders of earlier Roman con-
querors. At Ozogardana, from which the inhabitants fled before
Julian's troops, the podium from which the emperor Trajan
administered justice was on show.[17]

Soon, just north of the well-fortified town of Pirisabora
(modern al Anbar), at a place called Macepracta the army of
Julian entered a vast and fertile tract of Mesopotamia that was well
watered by irrigation canals and also contained a major waterway
joining the Euphrates to the Tigris. This was the Naharmalcha,
or King's River, that flowed from above Pirisabora in a southeasterly direction to meet the Tigris near Coche, which had taken
the place of the destroyed Seleuceia as Ctesiphon's sister-city on
the west bank of the Tigris.[18] The twin cities, which faced each
other across the river, were Julian's objective; and he quite sen-
sibly followed the Naharmalcha, when he reached it, so as to move
his fleet as expeditiously as possible over to the Tigris. Pirisabora
was besieged for two days. When it fell, the troops took possession of its supplies and put fire to it. Trouble arose in the army
at this time; but with evocations of the rich Persian spoils that lay
before them Julian succeeded in quelling mutinous and avaricious
troops, dissatisfied with a recent donative provided by the emperor.[19] The army advanced on its southeasterly course. A
Jewish community at Bithra (or, probably, Birtha, 'the fortress'
in Syriac) fled, and Julian's men burned this too.[20] Further to the
southeast near the King's River Maiozamalcha succumbed to an

---

[17] Amm. Marc. 24.1–2 on the organization of the army and its march. Trajan's
tribunal: 24.2.3.
[18] On the Naharmalcha, see L. Dilleman, *Syria* 38 (1961), 153–8 and F.
Paschoud on Zosimus 3.19 and 24, forthcoming in the *Collection Budé*. See also
two neglected Arabic texts which bear upon the course of this canal: Ṭabarī,
Ta'rīkh vol. 5 (Cairo, 1963), p. 204 (where *Kūfa* must certainly be corrected to
Kūqa) and Yaʿqūbī, *Kitāb al-buldān* (*Bibl. Geog. Arab.* VII), 321.13. These texts
show that the Nahr al-malik passed by Sābāṭ, near al–Madāʾin. For a discussion
of the problems of geography, see Paschoud on Zosimus 3.23 (on the town
Meinas Sabatha).
[19] Amm. Marc. 24.3.3–8.
[20] Zosimus 3.19 is the only source to mention this place.

adroit Roman manoeuvre by which a tunnel was built into the
city to avoid storming its walls.[21] The inhabitants discovered the
enemy erupting in their midst.

As Julian's forces drew near to the remains of Seleuceia and
were startled to be shown what were said to be relics of the
emperor Carus' disastrous campaign in those regions, Julian
himself discovered the existence of a Trajanic canal which had
been built to divert the waters of the King's River so that they
would flow into the Tigris above the twin cities of Coche and
Ctesiphon. The Tigris at that point was ill suited to accommodate
such an influx, which normally passed into an adequate channel
near Coche—much as the Rhône joins the Saône at Lyons. By
diverting the flow from the Euphrates both cities could be
seriously threatened with inundation, and at the same time the
Roman fleet could be brought to the Tigris above the cities
rather than at Coche itself. Trajan's canal, which Ammianus also
inadvertently calls the Naharmalcha,[22] had naturally been
dammed up, but Julian managed to open it and instantaneously
to terrify the cities of Ctesiphon and Coche.[23] This was a master
stroke.

To divert and refresh his men, many of whom must have still
been serving with the greatest reluctance, Julian held cavalry
games on the west bank of the Tigris in sight of the walls of
Ctesiphon.[24] These served also to display the size of his force and
to give pause to the Persian commanders. Meanwhile Julian
contemplated the storming of the important city that lay on the
opposite shore. He instructed the troops to cross the river by
night and to surprise the Persian soldiers in their quarters outside
the city. The success of this operation was offset by the extensive
pillaging to which Julian's men devoted their time after over-
whelming the enemy camp. Libanius believed that this search for

---

[21] Amm. Marc. 24.4.2–4; Libanius, *orat.* 18.235 ff. In Syriac *Māḥōz malkā*
means 'the king's fortified town'.   [22] Amm. Marc. 24.6.1.
[23] Libanius, *orat.* 18.247. In Zosimus 3.23 *Zochase* must be equated with *Coche*
(cf. F. Paschoud on this passage in the forthcoming Budé edition).
[24] Libanius 18.249; 1.133; Festus, *Brev.* 28. Cf. the scholion on *Anth. Pal.*
14.148.

spoils was the reason that the Romans lost their advantage in moving against Ctesiphon itself.[25] Certainly Julian quickly abandoned the effort to besiege the city. Very probably he was moved by the unnerving realization that the army of Procopius and Sebastianus had not arrived. Still worse, the forces of Shapur, the king of Persia, had not long been diverted and were now in the environs of Ctesiphon. Julian found himself in a dangerous situation, with his men now on the east bank of the Tigris and his fleet moored in the river. Any retreat had to be to the north, where Procopius and the others still were. The only waterway was the Diyala which branched off from the Tigris in a northward direction above Ctesiphon.

The emperor did a most astonishing thing when he abandoned the idea of besieging Ctesiphon. He ordered nearly all the ships in his fleet to be burned. In his funeral speech Libanius attempted (and Gibbon followed him in this) to defend Julian's action on the grounds of the great difficulty in moving ships upstream against the current of the Tigris and the undesirability of leaving the ships behind for the enemy. Also, Libanius declares with a straight face, by burning the ships Julian prevented idle soldiers from feigning sickness and sleeping on them.[26] But a year or more before Libanius wrote, Gregory of Nazianzus had heard that a clever Persian, pretending to be on bad terms with Shapur, had won Julian's confidence and promised to lead him by a short-cut to Julian's northern forces through the open country—avoiding the bending of the river. To facilitate movement away from the water he had persuaded the emperor to burn his fleet. This accomplished, the Persian disappeared, and Julian's troops soon found themselves confronting Shapur's army.[27] At about the same time as Gregory was writing, that is within a year or so of Julian's death, Ephraem wrote: 'And he—the emperor—commanded that the ships of victory be burnt, and his idols and demons were confounded by a trick.'[28]

[25] Libanius, *orat.* 18.255.   [26] Libanius, *orat.* 18.263.
[27] Greg. Naz., *orat.* 5.11–12 (Migne, *PG* 35.677).
[28] Ephraem, *Hymn against Julian* 3.15.

The success of the Persian trick was clearly not a point which Libanius wished to concede or mention, but both Festus by 372 and Ammianus two decades later confirm the Christian testimony.[29] Ammianus even adds that when Julian had discovered what had been done to him, as the ships were still blazing, he ordered the fire to be extinguished; but it was too late. Without the ships the Roman army had to struggle overland in an attempt to join the forces of Rome in northern Mesopotamia. After a brief trial of an inland route and encounters with Shapur's army, the Roman troops soon returned close to the Tigris above Ctesiphon. Though Libanius manages to conceal the fact, the army of Julian was in full retreat.

As early as Jerome and throughout the extant Christian tradition, it was a terrible desert, waterless and arid, in which Julian and his troops found themselves. Yet the inescapable facts of geography should long ago have prevented anyone from crediting such an account. The territory near Ctesiphon is green and fertile; there is no desert within reach. It is significant that the earliest Christian writers, Julian's contemporaries, knew nothing about wandering in a desert; nor, for that matter, did John Chrysostom. But with the help of Ammianus and Zosimus the legend can be understood and the truth disengaged,[30] for both writers agree that the Persians carried out an effective scorched-earth policy precisely to prevent the Romans from exploiting this fertile region. It was because of this that the troops went hungry in a dry land. The concord of Ammianus and Zosimus points again to Eunapius and the observations of Oribasius. Ammianus had, of course, been there and seen the terrain for himself. So had Oribasius. The sources before Ammianus make no mention of the scorched-earth policy, and that is transparently because they lacked any eyewitness report.

[29] Festus, *Brev.* 28 (on the date of Festus' work, cf. R. Tomlin, *Britannia* 5 [1974], 308 f.); Amm. Marc. 24.7.5. There is confusion as to whether one or more Persians were involved. See also Libanius, *orat.* 18.262–3; Zosimus 3.26 and 28.

[30] For the desert story, see Jerome, *Chron.* (Helm), p. 243; Philostorgius (Bidez–Winkelmann), p. 100; Sozomen 6.1.11. Cf. Ammianus 24.7.7 and Zosimus 3.28. See also the illuminating discussion in L. Dilleman, *Syria* 38 (1961), 123.

On 26 June 363, after considerable harassment by the Persians with their elephants, Julian encouraged his troops during an encounter in which the enemy was already turning to flight. As dust whirled round him on his horse, he was struck down by a cavalry spear that pierced his side and went into his groin.[31] In his haste he had forgotten to put on his breastplate and was equipped with only a shield for protection. Ephraem surmised that Julian, judging that he could neither be victorious nor escape from the Persians who surrounded him, deliberately exposed himself to a hostile spear as the only way out, and Gregory of Nazianzus says similarly that death in this way was his only hope.[32] Perhaps subconsciously there was some such motivation in Julian's desperate and reckless rush to encourage his men. It is hard to tell, especially since the tide of battle had turned when Julian was struck. The wounded emperor was carried to a tent, where Oribasius attended him. Whether he made a wise, philosophic discourse to his friends from his deathbed, as Ammianus would have us believe, is open to doubt. The Socratic parallel is too obvious. But late that night Julian's wound began to bleed effusively, and the emperor died.

The principal mystery, and crucial in the subsequent struggle between Christians and pagans, was the identity of the one who cast the fatal spear. Ephraem is vague, except that he considers the spear—'the lance of paradise, the lance of justice'—as carrying out God's will.[33] His silence implies that he took it for granted that the spear came from an enemy hand. Gregory, however, in 364 can already report four distinct traditions about Julian's demise: the spear came from (1) a Persian, (2) a barbarian camp-follower, (3) a Saracen (that is, a nomadic Arab in the forces of one side or the other), and (4) one of Julian's own soldiers, fed up with the campaign.[34] Libanius, writing his funeral speech in the next year, asserts confidently that it was a

---

[31] Amm. Marc. 25.3.6.
[32] Ephraem, *Hymn against Julian* 3.16; Greg. Naz., *orat.* 5.12 (Migne *PG* 35.677D).
[33] Ephraem, *Hymn against Julian* 3.14.
[34] Greg. Naz., *orat.* 5.13 (Migne *PG* 35.680A–B).

Roman who cast the spear and he implies, as Sozomen acknowledged in the following century, that it was a Roman Christian.[35] After the battle of Adrianople in 378 Libanius returned to the theme of Julian's death, for which in his view the Romans had been punished at Adrianople. In the speech on the avenging of Julian Libanius provides information he had obviously lacked at the time of his earlier comments. The assailant, he says, was a *Taiēnos* employed to murder Julian.[36] This is a striking detail, since *Taiēnos* can only be a Greek form of the Syriac *ṭayyāyē*, which matches the standard fourth-century use of the term *Sarakēnoi* or Saracens.[37] In other words, Libanius appears to have got his information from a local, Syriac-speaking informant.

It turns out that Libanius' later information, which he presents as simple fact, can be confirmed. Although Ammianus admits to knowledge of rumours of Roman guilt he prefers not to commit himself on the problem of the assassin of Julian;[38] and Zosimus is too sketchy to be helpful. It is in the ecclesiastical history of Philostorgius that the necessary trace of Eunapius' history can be found.[39] Philostorgius' use of Eunapius as a source is not in dispute, and for the death of Julian he alludes in some detail to Oribasius' treatment of the emperor after the shaft had been removed. With the recording of what intestinal material was extracted on the spear-point Philostorgius leaves us in no doubt that we are reading Oribasius' account as given by Eunapius. And Philostorgius states clearly and unambiguously that a Saracen threw the spear. What is more, this Saracen was a member of an auxiliary unit of Arab *kontophoroi* or cavalry spearmen on the *Persian* side. Philostorgius also answers a question ignored elsewhere: when Julian was struck, why did not someone immediately go after the attacker? Someone did, and beheaded him.

So Julian was most probably felled by a spear from the Persian army but from a Saracen hand. It had, of course, been convenient

---

[35] Libanius, *orat.* 18.274; cf. Sozomen 6.2.
[36] Libanius, *orat.* 24.6.
[37] Cf. G. W. Bowersock, *Gibbon et Rome* (1977), p. 209.
[38] Amm. Marc. 25.3.6 and 25.6.6.
[39] Philostorgius (Bidez-Winkelmann), p. 101.

for Libanius to be able to accuse the Christians either of doing the deed themselves or of having someone do it for them; and by the fifth century, as Sozomen shows, the Christians were by no means averse to taking the credit. It is ironic that we appear to recover our most authoritative pagan source in the pages of an ecclesiastical historian, though an unorthodox one, to be sure.

The death of Julian only confirmed a failure already obvious from the army's retreat. When the troops came to deliberate over the choice of a successor, it was clear that they were more interested in the personal character than the religion of the new emperor. For they first attempted to persuade the unimpeachable Salutius to accept the purple. Salutius was of course a pagan and remained one, but lacking Julian's abrasiveness and austere zeal he commanded wide respect among the Christians. When Salutius refused to receive the honour of the succession as well as the responsibility for extricating the Roman army, the election went to the Christian Jovian.[40] If Julian had indeed wanted Procopius, his kinsman, to succeed him, the fact evidently was a secret until 365 when Procopius tried unsuccessfully to seize power.

The retreat of the Roman forces under Jovian was achieved at the expense of large concessions to the Persians, as was inevitable. Eastern Mesopotamia was abandoned to the Sassanians, and Ephraem bewailed the evacuation of the great and often defended city of Nisibis. He saw the Persian standard hoisted over his old city, and outside its walls he saw the corpse of Julian on its way to burial in Tarsus.[41]

The fears of the Antiochenes came suddenly to an end. Instead of looking apprehensively to Tarsus as the new residence of the emperor, they viewed that city as his grave. The whole transformation which Julian had set in motion stopped abruptly with his death. He tried to reshape the world according to his personal vision, and that vision vanished with him. Even his more disreputable counsellors, Maximus and Priscus, did not suffer at once but only when they turned to new machinations under the

[40] Amm. Marc. 25.5.3–6.
[41] Ephraem, *Hymn against Julian* 3.1–2. Cf. Amm. Marc. 25.9.1.

succeeding emperors. There was no purge after Julian died; there were no trials at Chalcedon. The fanatic was gone, and there were few to regret him. In the orchestral fullness of later fourth-century rhetoric, the blaring tones of Libanius are a solo performance. Neither Eunapius nor Ammianus, with all their admiration for Julian, were under any illusion about his weaknesses or his ultimate failure. He demanded too much; he compromised unwisely and too little. But then, with advisers like Maximus and Priscus, it is perhaps not surprising that he found no way to translate into reality *ein längst entwöhntes Sehnen nach jenem stillen, ernsten Geisterreich.*

Appendix I

The Chronology of the Attempt to Rebuild the Jewish Temple

THE views of Michael Avi-Yonah on the chronology of the rebuilding of the temple at Jerusalem have recently been made accessible to a wider public through the publication of a valuable English edition, prepared by Avi-Yonah himself shortly before his death, of his work on the Jews in the time of the Talmud. In recent years Avi-Yonah's most mature thought on this subject was to be found only in the last Hebrew editions. In Chapter 8, part 5 of *The Jews of Palestine* (1976) interested readers will discover that Avi-Yonah argued for an extended period of work on the project, which he thought was not terminated until 27 May 363, several months after Julian had left Antioch. Since this dating is rejected in the present book, it may be worthwhile to say why.

Avi-Yonah relies on the following evidence for his dating:

(1) The fragment preserved by John the Lydian (*De mens.* IV, p. 110, 4 ed. Wünsch = Bidez, *Lettres* [ed. Budé] no. 134, p. 197): 'I am building with all zeal the new temple of the most high God.' Avi-Yonah (p. 199) describes this as a sentence from a letter 'written by the emperor in the course of his campaign'. He goes on to observe, 'This was apparently part of a proclamation addressed to the Jews of Mesopotamia and Babylonia.'

(2) An Ethiopic synaxarium (*Patrol. Orient.* I, p. 533) and the Syriac chronicle of 724 (*CSCO*, Script. Syr., III. IV, p. 104): Avi-Yonah writes (p. 200), 'The work must have gone on through April and May. On the 27th of May (according to the Abyssinian menology, i.e. in the month of "Iyar" according to the Syriac chronicle of 724) there occurred the event which led finally to the abandoning of the whole enterprise.'

As to the quotation preserved by John the Lydian, there is no indication whatever that it was addressed to Jews in Mesopotamia and Babylonia. All we are told is *graphōn Ioudaiois*, i.e. Julian was writing to Jews. John gives the time of composition as *hote pros Persas estrateueto*, 'when Julian was on campaign against the Persians'. This does indeed suggest composition after the departure from Antioch, but—should other testimony prove more compelling—it could conceivably be understood to refer to the whole period after Julian left Constantinople, since he went to Antioch as a base for his preparations to march against the Persians.

The oriental evidence invoked by Avi-Yonah is misreported and, upon inspection, irrelevant. The Ethiopic synaxarium records under 27 May that on that day the bodies of John the Baptist and Elisha were uncovered at Alexandria. The text goes on to tell a story according to which the bodies of the saints were disinterred in Palestine to permit the reconstruction of the Jewish temple as Julian had ordered. (A conflation with the Babylas incident seems likely here.) The bodies of John and Elisha were secretly transferred to Alexandria. Thus, the synaxarium only mentions the temple project as anterior, by an unspecified time, to 27 May. There is no mention of an earthquake nor of any circumstances causing work on the temple to cease.

The Syriac text does indeed record an earthquake in Iyar but it makes no mention of the Jewish temple. It views the earthquake as punishment for those peoples who had participated in Julian's paganism, and twenty-one cities are said to have suffered. Guidi's text in *CSCO* (p. 133 of the Syriac) shows that the manuscript dates the earthquake to 27 May, although Guidi supplements the text at this point with the words 'Julian was killed' and thereby wrenches the day of the month from its natural context in the Syriac. In the Latin translation (which is the only reference Avi-Yonah gives), Guidi's surgery is entirely concealed by the words 'Et die 27 huius mensis occisus est Iulianus'. It is possible that the date of 27 May 363 in both the Ethiopic and Syriac sources has some common origin. Whatever it was, the divergent purposes to which the date is put make any reliance upon it unwise. It is sufficient to observe here that neither text mentions at all the termination of the temple project.

Accordingly the only basis for assuming that work on the temple continued after Julian left Antioch is the phrase of John the Lydian, and even that is not absolutely compelling (nor, of course, is he the most reliable of commentators). The evidence for the abandonment of the project before Julian's departure is much too strong to be ignored. It is as follows:

(1) Ammianus XXIII. 1.2–3 dates the whole enterprise, including its failure, to the time when Julian was in Antioch. This is made very plain by the words which immediately follow the report of the termination of construction: *isdem diebus* introducing material belonging to the months in 363 when Julian was still at Antioch.

(2) In his long pastoral letter dating from the period at Antioch Julian refers to the fact that the Jewish temple has not been rebuilt although he observes that he had intended to have this done (Bidez, *Lettres* [ed. Budé], no. 89, p. 163 = 295C). The project had therefore been abandoned by the time of writing. There is no possibility that Julian's words (*anastēsasthai dienoēthēn*) could be construed to mean that it was his intention to rebuild the temple at some future time.

Finally it may be useful to mention some new and inconclusive evidence. In *Palestine Exploration Quarterly* 108 (1976), 103 ff. Sebastian Brock announced the existence of a Syriac letter allegedly by Cyril, Bishop of Jerusalem in Julian's reign, on the subject of the rebuilding of the temple. The full text exists only in a copy made in 1899, although part is said to appear in a British Library manuscript of the sixth century. Brock argues persuasively against the genuineness of the letter, but he thinks it may nevertheless be a fabrication of ancient times—of perhaps *ca.* A.D. 400.

The letter contains some curious and unparalleled details. It asserts that the actual rebuilding began on 18 May and was stopped by an earthquake on the night of 18 to 19 May. So late a commencement of work is scarcely credible, although the author of the letter states that 19 May in 363 was a Monday—which happens to be true. Among the horrendous episodes mentioned in connection with the earthquake is an automatic opening of the doors of the Jewish synagogue and the emission of a consuming fire. This phenomenon is explicitly connected by Gregory of Nazianzus with the temple doors; and Ephraem, who mentions the event, clearly implies, although he does not state explicitly, that the doors were part of the new temple. There are some topographical errors in the letter, which makes Cyril speak of a non-existent Church of the Confessors, a non-existent statue of Herod, and a non-existent grave of Jeremiah.

The letter includes a list of over twenty places affected by the earthquake (cf. the Syriac chronicle of 724 on twenty-one cities that suffered).

The 'new evidence' for Julian's temple project looks very much like an ancient forgery by some person with a good knowledge of the Syriac tradition but no direct knowledge of Jerusalem. The author probably knew Ephraem's invectives better than Gregory's, and he had some acquaintance with at least the antecedents of the chronicle of 724. It remains mysterious, however, where he discovered the date of 19 May or—it might be better to say—why he chose it. A developing tradition in the East of a late date for the termination of the temple project may possibly provide the correct explanation of John the Lydian's statement that Julian wrote to the Jews about the rebuilding when he was on campaign against the Persians.

It is worth noting particularly that the letter attributed to Cyril connects the earthquakes in Iyar with the end of the temple project. This the Syriac chronicle of 724 had conspicuously not done.

Appendix II

The Inscription at Ma'ayan Barukh

IN the *Israel Exploration Journal* 19 (1969), 170 ff. Dr. Avraham Negev published an important new inscription in honour of Julian. It was cut on a limestone column found near the Kibbutz Ma'ayan Barukh in the upper Jordan valley. The text as read and restored by Negev is as follows:

R[O]MANI ORBIS LIBERAT[ORI]
TEMPLORVM
[RE]STAVRATORI CVR
4 [IA]RVM ET REI PVBLICAE
RECREATORI BAR
BARORVM EXTINCTORI
D(OMINO) N(OSTRO) IOVLIANO
8 PERPETVO AVGVSTO
ALAMANNICO MAXIMO
FRANCICO MAXIMO
[SAR]MATICO MAXIMO
12 PONTIFICI MAXIMO PA
[TRI] PATRIAE FOENICVM
[SOC]IVS OB IMPET[RATA]
[BENEFICIA]

Negev proposed that this inscription be dated to the summer of 362, when Julian was in residence in Syria. The unparalleled expression *barbarorum extinctor* militates, however, against such a date. On these words Negev observed: 'No inscription of Julian known to us refers to wars against *barbari*. An inscription from Serdica (Dacia) [*CIL* III. 12333], enumerating the victories of Julian, has the following order: *Ger. maximo, Alamann. maximo, Fran. maximo, Sar. maximo.* It is thus possible that the *barbari* of our inscription stand for the *Germani* of the other.' This is not a necessary inference since *barbarorum extinctor* is a supplement to the honours recorded by the victory-titles, in which the Gallic successes are commemorated. It is placed in a series of more magnificent tributes appropriate to Julian as Augustus rather than Caesar.

As Augustus Julian had but one campaign against a frontier people who could be called *barbari*, and that was the Persian campaign. It is also worth emphasizing that in a Near-Eastern inscription the simple term *barbari* would in any case be most likely to refer to *eastern* barbarians. In the first months after his departure for Mesopotamia on 5 March 363, news of Julian's initial successes reached Antioch, as Libanius' two speeches of this period (15 and 16) prove. He calls the Persian adversaries precisely *barbaroi*. Observe, for example, Lib. 15.3, 15.17, and 16.9. Accordingly the inscription at Ma'ayan Barukh should be dated April or May, 363. It is an expression of homage from persons in the Near East who fully expected Julian's return later in the year and wished their allegiance to be on record.

The dedicants are indicated in lines 13–14 of the text as FOENICVM [. . .]IVS, restored by Negev to *Foenicum* [*soc*]*ius* with this comment: 'The barbaric form of the rendering of Phoenicia is not unusual, and an epitaph from Rome, of A.D. 205, has Foinicia. The *socius* must have been the *collegium* which dedicated the stone to the emperor.' *Foenicum* renders the genitive plural of *Phoenices* rather than *Phoenicia*, and *socius* is not a word for *collegium*. The dedicants were manifestly a body of Phoenicians, most probably the *koinon* or provincial assembly. Given the space available in line 14, we must certainly restore FOENICVM [COE]ṬVS. On the Phoenician *koinon* see J. Deininger, *Die Provinziallandtage der römischen Kaiserzeit* (1965), p. 88. For *coetus*, cf. Amm. Marc. 15.7.7: *coetus in unum quaesitus eiusdem legis cultorum* (*synodus ut appellant*); Sidonius, epist. 8.6.5: *acclamatum est ab omni Galliae coetu.*

Appendix III

The Author of *On the Gods and the Universe*

IN the *Revue des études anciennes* 65 (1963), 104 ff. Robert Étienne rightly distinguishes Flavius Sallustius, Julian's praetorian prefect of the Gauls and consul in 363, from Saturninius Secundus Salutius (often incorrectly called Sallustius), his old confidant and praetorian prefect of the East. Étienne then addresses himself to the identity of the author of the little Neo-Platonic treatise *On the Gods and the Universe*, ascribed in the manuscripts to a certain Sallustius. (This work is still best studied in the admirable edition of A. D. Nock [1925].) Some verses of Ausonius in praise of a Latin orator by the name of Alcimus Alethius are advanced as conclusive proof that Fl. Sallustius, the prefect of the Gauls, was the author of the treatise:

> Et Iulianum tu magis famae dabis
> quam sceptra, quae tenuit brevi.
> Sallustio plus conferent libri tui
> quam consulatus addidit.
> Aus. 16.3.21–4 (Schenkl)

The reference to a consulate proves that this Sallustius is the prefect of the Gauls—and that his name is therefore correctly spelt in the text. But *libri tui* refer manifestly to Alcimus' works. He presumably wrote a laudation of Sallustius as well as of Julian (cf. Courcelle, *Revue des études latines* 38 [1960], 413–24). The passage makes no allusion to Sallustius' own writings, if there were any. It proves nothing about the author of the Neo-Platonic treatise, whose content makes Salutius by far the more plausible candidate.

Bibliography

Significant contributions to historical scholarship on Julian since the late nineteenth century: this list does not include all works cited in the notes, nor do the notes include all works listed here.

Adler, M., 'The Emperor Julian and the Jews', *Jewish Quarterly Review* 5 (1893), 622 ff.

Allard, P., *Julien l'Apostat* (2nd ed.; 1902–3).

Andreotti, R., 'L'opera legislativa ed amministrativa dell' Imperatore Giuliano', *Nuova Rivista Storica* 14 (1930), 342 ff.

—, *Il regno dell' Imperatore Giuliano* (1936).

Arce, J. J., 'Algunas problemas de la numismatica del emperador Fl. Cl. Iulianus', *Archivo español de arqueología* 45–7 (1972–4), 477 ff.

—, 'Reconstrucciones de templos paganos en epoca del emperador Juliano', *Rivista storica dell'antichità* 5 (1975), 201 ff.

Asmus, R., *Julian and Dion Chrysostomos* (1895).

—, *Julians Galiläerschrift* (1904).

—, 'Kaiser Julians Misopogon und seine Quelle', *Philologus* 76 (1920), 266 ff. and 77 (1921), 109 ff.

Avi-Yonah, M., 'The Emperor Julian and the Jews', in Avi-Yonah, *The Jews of Palestine* (1976), pp. 185 ff.

Balty, J. and J. Ch., 'Julien et Apamée: Aspects de la restauration de l'hellénisme et de la politique antichrétienne de l'empereur', *Ann. Lib. Univ. Besançon* 166 (1974), 267 ff.

Barnes, T. D., 'A Law of Julian', *Classical Philology* 69 (1974), 288 ff.

—, 'The *Epitome de Caesaribus* and its Sources', *Classical Philology* 71 (1976), 258 ff.

Baynes, N. H., 'The Early Life of Julian the Apostate', *Journal of Hellenic Studies* 45 (1925), 251 ff.

—, 'The Death of Julian the Apostate in a Christian Legend', *Journal of Roman Studies* 27 (1937), 22 ff.

Béranger, J., 'Julien l'apostat et l'hérédité du pouvoir impérial', *Antiquitas* Reihe 4: *Bonner Historia-Augusta-Colloquium* 1970 (1972), 75 ff.

Bidez, J., 'L'évolution de la politique de l'empereur Julien en matière religieuse,' *Bulletin de l'Académie Royale de Belgique*, Classe des lettres 7 (1914), 406 ff.

—, *La tradition manuscrite et les éditions des discours de Julien* (1929).

—, *La vie de l'empereur Julien* (1930).

Bischoff, B., and Nörr, D., 'Eine unbekannte Konstitution Kaiser Julians', *Bayerische Akademie der Wissenschaften*, Phil.-Hist. Klasse, Abh. N. F. 58 (1963).

Blockley, R. C., 'Constantius Gallus and Julian as Caesars of Constantius II', *Latomus* 31 (1972), 433 ff.

von Borries, E., 'Iulianus Apostata', Pauly-Wissowa's *Real-Encyclopädie* 19 (1917), cols. 26 ff.

Bowersock, G. W., 'Gibbon and Julian', *Gibbon et Rome à la lumière de l'historiographie moderne, Publications de la Faculté des Lettres de l'Université de Lausanne*, XXII (1977), pp. 191–217.

Brock, Sebastian P., 'The Rebuilding of the Temple under Julian: A New Source', *Palestine Exploration Quarterly* 108 (1976), 103 ff.

Brok, M. A. F., *De Perzische Expeditie van Kaiser Julianus volgens Ammianus Marcellinus* (1959).

Browning, R., *The Emperor Julian* (1975).

Büttner-Wobst, T., 'Der Tod des Kaisers Julian', *Philologus* 51 (1892), 561 ff.

Calza, R., *Iconografia romana imperiale da Carausio a Giuliano* (1972).

Cameron, A., 'An Alleged Fragment of Eunapius', *Classical Quarterly* n.s. 13 (1963), 232 ff.

Chalmers, W., 'Eunapius, Ammianus, and Zosimus', *Classical Quarterly* n.s. 10 (1960), 152 ff.

Conduché, D., 'Ammien Marcellin et la mort de Julien', *Latomus* 24 (1965), 359 ff.

Croissant, J., 'Un nouveau discours de Thémistius', *Serta Leodiensia* (1930), 22 ff.

Cumont, F., *Sur l'authenticité de quelques lettres de Julien* (1889).

De Jonge, P., 'Scarcity of Corn and Corn Prices in Ammianus Marcellinus', *Mnemosyne* 1 (1948), 238 ff.

Dilleman, L., 'Ammien Marcellin et les Pays de l'Euphrate et du Tigre', *Syria* 38 (1961), 87 ff.

Downey, G., 'Julian the Apostate at Antioch', *Church History* 8 (1939), 303 ff.

—, 'The Economic Crisis at Antioch under Julian the Apostate', *Studies in Roman Economic and Social History in Honor of Allan Chester Johnson* (1951), 312 ff.

—, 'The Emperor Julian and the Schools', *Classical Journal* 53 (1957), 97 ff.

—, 'Julian the Philosopher, A.D. 361–363', in Downey, *A History of Antioch in Syria* (1961), pp. 380 ff.

Elmer, G., 'Die Kupfergeldreform unter Julianus Philosophus,' *Numismatische Zeitschrift* 70 (1937), 25 ff.

Ensslin, W., 'Kaiser Julians Gesetzgebungswerk und Reichsverwaltung', *Klio* 18 (1923), 104 ff.

128 *Bibliography*

Étienne, R., 'Flavius Sallustius et Secundus Salutius', *Revue des études anciennes* 65 (1963), 104 ff.

Festugière, A. J., 'Julien à Macellum', *Journal of Roman Studies* 47 (1957), 53 ff.

—, *Antioche païenne et chrétienne* (1959).

de Gaiffier, B., '"Sub Iuliano Apostata" dans le martyrologe romain', *Analecta Bollandiana* 74 (1956), 9 f.

Geffcken, J., *Kaiser Julianus* (1914).

Gigli, G., *Giuliano l'Apostata* (1960).

Gilliard, F. D., 'Notes on the Coinage of Julian the Apostate', *Journal of Roman Studies* 54 (1964), 135 ff.

Goffart, W., 'Did Julian Combat Venal *Suffragium*?' *Classical Philology* 65 (1970), 145 ff.

Gramatopol, M., 'L'apothéose de Julien l'Apostat et de Flavia Helena sur le Grand Camée de Roumanie', *Latomus* 34 (1965), 873 ff.

Hahn, I., 'Der ideologische Kampf um den Tod Julians des Abtrünnigen', *Klio* 38 (1960), 225 ff.

Hauser-Meury, Marie-Madeleine, *Prosopographie zu den Schriften Gregors von Nazianz* (1960).

Kabiersch, J., *Untersuchungen zum Begriff der Philanthropie bei dem Kaiser Julian* (1960).

Kaegi, W. E., 'The Emperor Julian's Assessment of the Significance and Function of History', *Proceedings of the American Philosophical Society* 108 (1964), 29 ff.

—, 'Research on Julian the Apostate 1945–1964', *Classical World* 58 (1965), 229 ff.

—, 'Domestic Military Problems of Julian the Apostate', *Byzantinische Forschungen* 2—Festschrift Dölger (1967), 247 ff.

—, 'The Emperor Julian at Naïssus', *L'antiquité classique* 44 (1975), 161 ff.

Kent, J. P. C., 'An Introduction to the Coinage of Julian the Apostate', *Numismatic Chronicle* 19 (1959), 109 ff.

Koch, W., 'Comment l'empereur Julien tâcha de fonder une église païenne', *Revue belge de philologie et d'histoire* 6 (1927), 123 ff.; 7 (1928), 49 ff.; 7 (1928), 511 ff.; 7 (1928), 1363 ff.

Labriola, I., *Giuliano l'Apostata-Autobiografia* (1975).

Lacombrade, Chr., 'Notes sur les Césars de l'empereur Julien', *Pallas* 11 (1962), 47 ff.

—, 'L'empereur Julien émule de Marc-Aurèle', *Pallas* 14 (1967), 9 ff.

Leipoldt, J., 'Der römische Kaiser Julian in der Religionsgeschichte', *Sitzungsberichte der Sächs. Akad. der Wissenschaften* 110, 1, 1964.

Lewy, J. H., 'The Emperor Julian and the Rebuilding of the Temple', in Hebrew, *Olamot Nefgashim* (1969), pp. 221 ff.

Mau, D., *Die Religionsphilosophie Kaiser Julians in seinen Reden auf König Helios und die Göttermutter* (1907).

Mueller-Seidel, I., 'Die Usurpation Julians des Abtrünnigen im Lichte seiner Germanenpolitik', *Historische Zeitschrift* 180 (1955), 225 ff.

Negev, A., 'The Inscription of the Emperor Julian at Ma'ayan Barukh', *Israel Exploration Journal* 19 (1969), 170 ff.

Neumann, K. J., 'Das Geburtsjahr Kaiser Iulians', *Philologus* 50 (1891), 761 f.

Norman, A. F., 'Magnus in Ammianus, Eunapius, and Zosimus', *Classical Quarterly* n.s. 7 (1957), 129 ff.

—, *Libanius' Autobiography* (1965).

Pack, R. A., 'Notes on the *Caesars* of Julian', *Transactions of the American Philological Association* 77 (1946), 151 ff.

—, 'Two Sophists and Two Emperors', *Classical Philology* 42 (1947), 17 ff.

—, 'Ammianus Marcellinus and the *Curia* of Antioch', *Classical Philology* 48 (1953), 80 ff.

Petit, P., *Libanius et la vie municipale à Antioche au IV siècle après J.–C.* (1955).

Radinger, C., 'Das Geburtsdatum des Kaisers Iulian Apostata', *Philologus* 50 (1891), 761.

Ricciotti, G., *Julian the Apostate*, trans. M. J. Costelloe (1960).

Richtsteig, F., 'Einige Daten aus dem Leben Kaisers Julians', *Philologische Wochenschrift* 51 (1931), 128 ff.

Ridley, R. T., 'Notes on Julian's Persian Expedition', *Historia* 22 (1973), 317 ff.

Rosen, K., 'Beobachtungen zur Erhebung Julians', *Acta Classica* 12 (1969), 121 ff.

Rostagni, A., *Giuliano l'Apostata* (1920).

Schemmel, F., 'Die Schulzeit des Kaisers Julian', *Philologus* 82 (1927), 455 ff.

Seeck, O., *Die Briefe des Libanius zeitlich geordnet* (1906).

Szidat, J., *Historischer Kommentar zu Ammianus Marcellinus XX–XXI, Teil I: Die Erhebung Iulians*, Historia Einzelschrift, Heft 31 (1977).

Thompson, E. A., 'Three Notes on Julian in 361 A.D.', *Hermathena* 62 (1943), 90 ff.

—, *The Historical Work of Ammianus Marcellinus* (1947).

Vogt, J., 'Kaiser Julian und das Judentum', *Morgenland* 30 (1939), 46 ff.

—, 'Kaiser Julian über seinen Oheim Constantin den Grossen', *Historia* 4 (1955), 339 ff.

Weis, B., *Das Restitutions—Edict Kaiser Julians* (1933).

Index

153